Selling Tax Strategies

THE FINANCIAL GRAVITY GUIDE TO BUILDING YOUR BUSINESS BY CUTTING YOUR CLIENTS' TAXES

Edward A. Lyon, JD, CTM

John D. Pollock, CTM

Tax Master Network
www.TaxMasterNetwork.com

Selling Tax Strategies
The Financial Gravity Guide To Building Your Business By Cutting Your Clients' Taxes

Copyright © 2018 by Financial Gravity

Contents

Introduction   **4**

The Tax Business Is Broken   **9**

Why Accountants Suck   9

Why Financial Advisors Suck   11

Technology is Making Things Worse   16

Here's the Solution   23

How to Build Your Tax Planning Business   **27**

Prospecting for Tax Savings   27

Craft a Compelling Message   34

The Elevator Speech   40

How to Open Cases   42

How to Close Tax Plan Sales   46

How to Fire the Old Accountant   52

How to Sell Current Clients   53

Establishing Your Value to Your Clients   **57**

Value Pricing for Tax Planning   67

Tax Strategy Survey   **71**

Spotlight on Tax Deferral   72

Spotlight on Retirement Income   79

Spotlight on Insurance Products   83

Spotlight on Mutual Funds   90

Where to Go From Here   **94**

Dip Your Toe Into the Water   95

The Fractional Family Office®   95

Introduction

"A dog who thinks he is man's best friend is a dog who obviously has never met a tax lawyer."

Fran Lebowitz

This is a book that really shouldn't have to exist. (And how's THAT for an opening line?)

Americans hate paying taxes. It's coded into our national DNA! We fought for independence from England, in large part, to stop King George III from taxing us without our consent. (We've learned since then that taxation with representation isn't a whole lot better, but that's a different story.) We waited until the Civil War to experiment with an income tax, and dropped it as soon as we could afford to. Tax "protesters" are still whining that the 16th Amendment, authorizing the current form of federal income tax, is somehow illegitimate. And it's telling that even in today's hyperpartisan Congress, the one thing Republicans could accomplish during Donald Trump's first year in office was . . . cut income taxes.

So selling tax savings ought to be easy, right? After all, everyone wants to pay less. It ought to be like selling funnel cakes at the state fair!

If you're a CPA, enrolled agent, or financial advisor, though, you've realized that's not the case. Even tax savings don't sell themselves. Selling anything is hard if you don't have a system for doing it. And there are very few systems out there specifically focusing on selling tax savings. This book fills that gap, with systems that we've developed over the last thirteen years in both the accounting and financial services worlds.

Taxes are big business, to be sure. IBISWorld, which bills itself as the country's largest provider of industry and procurement research, reports that tax preparation services generated $11 billion in revenue in 2017. Full-service accounting firms (which, of course, provide far more services than just tax preparation) generated $110 billion. And financial advisors generated another $56 billion in fees and commissions.

If those numbers sound like opportunity knocking, well, they should. They prove that Americans are willing to pay–and pay handsomely–for someone to guide them through the Byzantine collection of statutes, regulations, IRS guidance, and case law that we laughingly refer to as a tax "system." (And what did the folks in Byzantium do to get such a bad rap, anyway?)

Of course, the fact that we can spend so much on those services tells us there's already plenty of competition. That means we have to work to be more than just "me too."

The playwright Tennessee Williams has a great quote that sums up the biggest challenge to succeeding in any business. "There are only three cities in America," he once said. "New York, San Francisco, and New Orleans. Everyplace else is Cleveland."

Now I apologize if you're from Cleveland and I've just insulted your beloved Mistake by the Lake Rock and Roll Capital of the World. Williams could have just as easily picked St. Louis, Indianapolis, or Milwaukee to mock. The point is, if you want to thrive in the crowded tax business, you can't be like everybody else. And adding "EA" or "CPA" to your name isn't going to help you stand out.

This book is your step-by-step guide to doing just that:

- We'll identify what's wrong with the tax industry today and why it doesn't deliver what clients really want.

- We'll identify how advancing technology is poised to disrupt, reinvent, and even destroy the current ways that you manage your work and do business with your clients.

- We'll discuss how to use tax savings to identify and attract clients who are ready to commit to doing business now.

- We'll give you word-for-word scripts and step-by-step systems for opening conversations and selling services.

- We'll give you a powerful analogy for explaining how the tax system works that immediately sets you apart from your competition.

- We'll help you build a value-based brand that emphasizes relationships over transactions.

- We'll challenge some of the conventional financial wisdom that actually costs clients taxes they shouldn't have to pay.

- We'll walk you through specific tax-planning challenges with strategies for emphasizing the unique value you can bring to your clients.

- Finally, we'll reveal a new business model that lets you offer your affluent clients a new level of service previously reserved for the ultra-wealthy.

Selling tax and accounting services is hard. Lots of bright, hard-working accountants open the doors to their own practice, then slink back into working for "the man" when they find they can't make it fly. Selling life insurance is so hard that only one out of ten people who try it manage to succeed. Selling and managing investments is a constant challenge in a world where there's always somebody with "a better track record" clients can turn to.

What if there were a way that you could skip all those headaches by selling clients free money from the government? There is . . . and this book opens that door.

About the Author: Ed Lyon

I've spent thirteen years helping accountants use proactive tax planning to build their businesses. I'm convinced the secret of my success is that I'm not an accountant to begin with!

In 1991, I earned my law degree from the University of Cincinnati. I loved taxes (really!), but I knew I didn't want to work in a stuffy law firm slicing and dicing my time in tenth-of-an-hour increments and grubbing for billable hours. So I set out on a career that took me from the National Underwriter Company (where I wrote and edited tax-oriented publications for insurance agents and financial advisors), to Merrill Lynch (where I washed out because I hadn't yet learned any of the lessons I teach in this book!), to Ohio National

Life Insurance (where I helped agents market retirement plans), to finally starting my own tax practice.

I knew from the start that I wanted to focus my business on pro-active tax planning. And I've always enjoyed public speaking—I love being the smart guy at the front of the room. So I created an information product called Instant Tax Relief that consisted of a three-ring binder with one-page modules outlining hundreds of tax-saving strategies, forms and templates for implementing tools like the Section 105 medical expense reimbursement plan, and a personal consultation to help buyers identify exactly which strategies would save them the most. I started booking seminars where I could sell that product. And I saw how hungry the audiences were for more than just the traditional tax-preparation services they were getting from their accountants.

After a bit of time, I realized I could take my Instant Tax Relief system and customize it for specific clients. One of them included my friend and neighbor Keith VandeStadt, a CPA who gave thanks every day that he had gone into systems consulting rather than tax or audit, and who had never prepared his own taxes. And as we sat at the bar at Teller's restaurant on Cincinnati's Hyde Park Square to present his plan, I told him I thought it would be fun to turn the material into an interactive software so that accountants across the country could prepare plans for their clients. He said, "I think I could do that," and TaxCoach Software was born.

We launched TaxCoach in 2005. Accountants across the country loved the concept. They just didn't know how to sell it. So we added a whole suite of marketing tools to the system: letters, web content, seminar kits, and even a done-for-you weekly email called The Networker. I started coaching individual accountants one-on-one, and we began hosting regional and national meetings where members could meet each other to share their successes and failures in a supportive, nurturing environment.

In 2015, TaxCoach merged with my co-author John Pollock's company, Financial Gravity. In 2018, we transformed the TaxCoach system into the Tax Master Network®. At the end of this book, you'll learn how that merger and repositioning have created a whole new opportunity for professionals like you to use tax planning to build your business!

About the Author: John Pollock

I'm an entrepreneur, above and beyond anything else.

I tried college and got bored, so I just got out into the world and hustled. After corporate jobs from putting burgers on a conveyor belt (I worked at Burger King, but I didn't actually flip the burgers) to selling for a MoneyMailer franchisee and an Inc. 500 company. (This was before Inc. realized they can sell more stuff if 5000 made the list instead of 500).

I got into insurance, and later wealth management, because I had a knack for the numbers and I was tired of working for someone else that was intimidated by my drive. After getting hammered by taxes while I was hearing on the news that "rich people don't pay their fair share," I reached out to the CPA field for help.

But I didn't get the answers I wanted. Instead, I heard, "you make what you make, so you pay what you have to pay." This started me on the journey I'm now on. I met Ed Lyon; we joined forces, and now we're saving business owners across the country from unnecessary taxes.

I'm doing it as the CEO of the now public company Financial Gravity Companies, Inc. (OTCQB: FGCO). We need your help to change how businesses operate and get them the money that is rightly theirs, so that they can create jobs and–most importantly–continue to make cool stuff for us to buy and use!

The Tax Business Is Broken

Why Accountants Suck

We'll start our discussion of the broken tax industry by looking at what accountants and financial advisors really do for their clients, and why that creates opportunities for you. We'll start with accountants and tax preparers. But if you're a financial advisor reading this book, don't skip ahead. You'll need to understand how most accountants disappoint their clients, so you can position yourself as a credible alternative!

Here's the problem with most accountants when it comes to taxes. They focus all their time on recording the history their clients give them. They put the "right" numbers" in the "right" boxes on the "right" forms and get them filed by the "right" deadlines.

But then they call it a day and move on to the next return. By that point, there's not much they can do to change that history (other than making an occasional IRA or SEP contribution). So they don't even try to change it before moving on to the next return!

It's like driving a car using just the rear-view mirror instead of the windshield. You would never try and back your car out of the garage, back it down the driveway to the street, and back it all the way to work. (Would you?) So why think clients would be happy if that's how you treat their taxes?

Now, recording history is important, and there is value in doing it right. Lots of people want to know how much your clients make in a year—clients themselves, the IRS, the bank that holds their business loans, their kids' college financial aid offices, and maybe a jealous ex-spouse or two.

But clients don't just want to know how much they owe. They want to know how to pay less.

Burn that last paragraph into your brain. Clients don't just want to know how much they owe. They want to know how to pay less.

Unfortunately, most accountants aren't giving it to them!

Accountants don't spend all their time recording history, of course. Plenty of them do year-end projections for their clients. This involves sitting down with a calculator and income statement, estimating how much the client will owe based on the best estimate of those numbers, and adjusting the client's January 15 estimated tax payment up or down based on how those numbers look.

They call that "planning" because it helps clients plan for a bigger or smaller tax bill. And there's real value in planning to avoid an ugly April 15 surprise! But this sort of year-end process isn't really "planning" at all–it's projection. The accountants who do this for their clients are just projecting more accurate scenarios to determine how much the client will eventually owe. And they generally complete the entire exercise without even considering ways to reduce that new, more accurate number.

Having said that, some clients will press for more proactive ways to pay less. And that leads to the world's most common tax "planning" recommendation: "buy a new car/truck/tractor/bulldozer/building for your business." Some insiders have dubbed this "yellow fever" because Caterpillar brand equipment is painted yellow. (Don't worry, John Deere fans, your green equipment saves you just as much in green for every dollar you spend as a Caterpillar.)

Other common year-end planning recommendations include establishing retirement plans, making charitable contributions, prepaying state/local taxes, and similar last-minute moves to take income off a client's return.

This, at last, is "planning." It's more than just telling clients how much they owe. It's a proactive step to help them pay less by changing the client's final year-end history.

Unfortunately, this sort of informal, last-minute planning isn't enough to set you apart from your competition. And, for reasons we'll discuss later, your clients probably won't even appreciate it. It's also not enough to demonstrate your real value to your client.

Finally, if you wait until the last minute to do your tax planning for your clients, you'll leave a ton of wasted money on the table for the IRS to take.

John's Note: It's almost like the accounting industry has be-
come a bunch of factories dedicated to putting numbers in box-
es, and the accountant can't afford to care about YOUR boxes
because the assembly line is running, and more numbers
have to be put into the boxes. He might steal a few seconds
away from the factory floor to point out planning opportunities.
But he isn't going to recommend something that messes with
the factory, and he isn't going to recommend something that
slows down the process with irregular forms or "uncomfortable"
strategies. ("Uncomfortable" here is usually code for "we don't
know how to do it and we don't want to mess with figuring it
out.") They just want you happy enough to keep giving them
the work to keep the factory busy and the conveyor belts mov-
ing.

Accountants should want to be in the advisory business. Why?
Because clients want them creating whatever keeps more
money in their pockets, not just what keeps the factory running
smoothly for the vendor they are paying.

Why Financial Advisors Suck

At the risk of stereotyping here, financial advisors as a group tend
to be more proactive than accountants. Financial advisors—the
ones who succeed long-term, at least—tend to be more comfortable with sales and with ~~pushing~~ gently guiding clients to make
decisions and take action. They tend to be "top-down" thinkers who
focus on the forest, rather than the trees. They aren't burdened by
the same need to manage details, accrue the accruals, and make
the balance sheets actually balance as accountants.

But make no mistake, advisors suck, too. In fact, in their own way,
they suck even worse than accountants!

For starters, financial advisors tend not to have the same depth of
technical knowledge when it comes to taxes as accountants. Sure,
they know the basics. Any life insurance agent can tell you the
basic tax rules for life insurance and annuities. Most investment
advisors can explain why an index mutual fund is more tax-efficient than an actively-managed fund. And a technically sophisti-

cated Certified Financial Planner might even be able to speak to advanced planning using charitable trusts, or using oil and gas partnerships as part of a diversified, tax-efficient portfolio.

But few financial advisors have the deep technical knowledge and perspective to analyze and evaluate tax strategies for clients outside their investment portfolios.

Let's say your client is a self-employed interior designer, netting $200,000 per year, operating her business as a sole proprietorship. You know that opening a SEP account could let her save $40,000 per year and avoid tax on that current income. Assuming she files singly and takes the standard deduction, that'll save her almost $12,000 in income tax. Sounds like a win, right?

But what if she reorganized her business as an S corp and paid herself a salary of $80,000? That would save her $7,500 in FICA, right off the bat. Best of all, she's not just deferring the tax like she is with the SEP. (Remember, she'll still owe taxes when she pulls it out of the account in retirement.) And she could still establish a Solo 401(k) and defer $38,500, plus more if she's above age 50.

Most financial advisors also wouldn't feel comfortable exploring a home office deduction, evaluating buy versus lease options for the pricey SUV she uses to impress clients, or renting her home to herself for up to 14 days of tax-free income per year.

So, financial advisors can be more proactive than their accountant friends. They can be technical experts within their own "lane" when it comes to specific financial and investment products and strategies. But they generally don't have the broader holistic perspective that clients need to really make the most of their tax-planning opportunities.

That leads to what we call the "hammer/nail problem" and the "suitability problem."

You've certainly heard the old saying that if the only tool you have is a hammer, everything looks like a nail. Well, sometimes financial advisors take their favorite products and try to position them as the solution to problems they really aren't suited for.

Take life insurance, for example. As we'll discuss later, permanent life insurance is a wonderful tax-saving tool. There's no deduction for premiums going into the policy. But cash values accumulate tax-deferred no matter how you invest them. And you can take money from the policy tax free in the form of loans and withdrawals. It's like a Roth IRA with no contribution limits or eligibility restrictions. This tax treatment makes life insurance a tremendously powerful retirement-savings vehicle.

But life insurance can be pricey. If you're a pudgy 60-year-old smoker, you're maxing out your 401(k), and you want to stuff a bunch of extra money into your savings, you'll spend a fair amount just paying for the death benefit before you can access that tax deferral goodness. If you need the death benefit, that might justify the trade off. But if you've already got all the coverage you need, we can probably find you a better place to put those savings.

Many advisors have abandoned looking for clients to buy products and started looking for clients to buy strategies. They look for clients with specific tax problems, then help those clients solve those problems. We've met advisors specializing in cash-balance pension plans, charitable trusts and LLCs, closely-held insurance companies, IC-DISCs, and similar advanced solutions.

These strategies are all very powerful and effective in the right situation. But finding prospects who are really suited for them can be difficult. And yes, you can always "pivot" when you discover that what your CHIC prospect really needs is a charitable remainder trust. But you'll find it easier to market yourself if you look for prospects who are simply feeling pain over their tax bill—then offer them a complete toolbox of solutions for any problem you encounter.

BAD PRODUCTS/STRATEGIES

Finally, the tax and investment world is full of just-plain-bad strategies that really aren't suited for anyone. But unscrupulous salespeople know that some clients will do almost anything to avoid taxes, and they're perfectly willing to use that pain to push unsuitable products and strategies. Typically, these trade some level of tax relief today for an even greater tax bill or investment risk down the road.

Let's say your client is a 45-year-old middle manager at the local paper mill or auto-parts manufacturer. He's finally worked his way out of the cubicles and into a real office . . . just before learning he's part of the latest "rightsizing." He's feeling a little burned right now. He sure doesn't want to go back to work for "the man!"

So now he's looking at buying a franchise and building a sandwich empire. He's got the cash to do it, in his 401(k). The only problem is, drawing the money out of the account will mean paying a hefty tax bill, plus a 10% penalty for the early withdrawal.

But there's an escape hatch – a tool that lets him get the money for the franchise out of the account without paying the tax or the penalty. It's called a Rollover for Business Startup, or ROBS. Briefly, it lets him establish a C corporation, adopt a 401(k) plan for the corporation, roll his balance from his old employer's plan into the new C corporation's plan, use it to buy stock in the C corporation, then finally use the money in the C corporation to finance the franchise.

That sounds like a great solution. The client has a problem—he needs money to start his new business. He has the money, but he can't use it without paying a huge tax bill. The ROBS lets him access the money without paying the tax bill. Everyone wins, right?

But here's the problem. The ROBS creates a bunch of new problems and dangers down the road. And in all too many cases, those new problems outweigh the benefit the client gets from solving the up-front tax problem:

- The ROBS has to operate as a bona fide retirement plan for all the company's employees, with all the technical requirements and red tape that a qualified plan requires. If the ROBS fails that challenge, it can be disqualified, and the owner can be forced to pay immediate tax on the entire account balance. Ouch!

- The new business has to operate as a C corporation. If it loses money up front, like many startups do, those losses are locked inside the corporation until it shows taxable income to offset. The owner can't use those losses to offset income from a spouse or another job.

- The owner can draw income from the new business only in the form of salary (taxed at the client's top marginal rate and subject to FICA too), or dividends (subject to tax at both corporate and personal levels).

- If the business succeeds and the client eventually sells it, the gains on that sale that would have been taxed at lower capital gains rates (if the client hadn't used the ROBS) go back into the retirement plan to be taxed at higher ordinary income rates. The client also loses the chance to benefit from stepped-up basis at death. (Well, his heirs do.)

- If the business eventually fails—like a majority of business startups—the client can't take the capital loss because it's locked inside the retirement plan. Even worse, there goes the client's retirement savings!

So, what do you think? Yes, the ROBS can help clients solve the problem of finding money to start their business. But it can cost them big-time down the road. Plenty of Tax Master Network® members have run into clients who have been ROBbed by this strategy, and almost unanimously they recommend staying as far away as possible!

> *John's Note: As bad as this is, Ed is underselling just how bad this really is. That's because we can accomplish the same goal as the ROBS with other products and services that pay a representative more and are better for the client in both the short run and the long run, regardless of the outcome. And if that wasn't enough, the other, higher-paying strategies reduce the overall risk to the business owner and protect the retirement nest-egg. The only reason someone sells a ROBS strategy is because that's the only thing they sell. They aren't advising; they're selling. This "advice vs selling" issue is epidemic in the financial services industry.*

This is actually a common problem that we'll discuss as we walk through the rest of this book. You don't do clients any favors if solving tax problems today means creating bigger problems tomorrow. This is something that both accountants and advisors have to watch out for. But the flip side of that coin is the opportunity to show clients you've considered those dangers and made yourself even more valuable. We'll talk about those opportunities more when we discuss how you demonstrate your value to your clients. Get ready to hear that phrase a lot!

John's Note: Let me sum up why advisors suck, since I've been in that specific industry for 15 years and hold all the necessary licenses to suck with them. I've also attended hundreds of hours of Continuing Education, been to countless conferences and even been on the award trips with the "advisor elite." Overall, most advisors sell one of three things: a product (such as an annuity, a REIT, or a mutual fund), a strategy (401k, Defined Benefit Plan, tax-free retirement), or a transaction (they sell it, you buy it, they get paid). This model is easier to implement because it lets the advisor learn one thing; launch their "hammer" into the market to look for a "nail." That's much easier than collecting loads of information, then fumbling around in the toolbox for the right tool (A screwdriver? A wrench?) for whatever problem the client needs to solve. It comes down to the fact that the financial services industry can be exceptionally lucrative and it trains "advisors" to be lazy and sell one very profitable thing.

Technology is Making Things Worse

Now let's look at another challenge you face in your quest to build a standout tax or financial business – the challenge of changing technology.

If your kids are old enough to be online, you've probably told them not to talk to strangers on the Internet. When you were growing up, your parents told you not to get in strangers' cars. Now, your phone has an app that lets you call a stranger ... on the Internet ... to get in their car.

Customers love it. Uber has just creamed taxi companies. In 2014, New York City taxi medallions sold for as much as $1.4 million. By 2017, when every native and tourist had installed Uber on their phone, medallion prices had plunged as low as $150,000.

But Uber is more than just a way to get from Point A to Point B. It's become a basis for all sorts of "Uber for X" companies in other industries. There's Wag (Uber for dog walkers), Heal (Uber for doctors), Minibar (Uber for alcohol), Eaze (Uber for medical marijuana), and even Plowz (you guessed it . . . Uber for snowplows).

That's pretty impressive for a company that launched in 2009. But Uber isn't resting on its existing success. It's investing in self-driving technology (to eliminate the cost of paying those pesky drivers) and vertical take-off and landing technology (to avoid that pesky traffic). None of that may sound directly relevant to you and your business—but it illustrates just how quickly a new technology can come out of nowhere to disrupt existing commerce.

Amazon started out in 1994 as an online bookseller. It went public in 1997 and didn't turn a profit until 2001. Now, it's racing to become the world's first trillion-dollar company, and founder Jeff Bezos is the richest man in the world. (Seriously, when Bezos walks into his neighborhood Applebees, the average customer is a billionaire.)

Amazon has disrupted retailing in every market it enters. In 2017, when Amazon acquired Whole Foods, Amazon's stock went up by more than the value of the company it had just bought. That's because the market assumed Amazon would introduce efficiencies to push Whole Foods' value up even more. Later that year, rival Kroger's stock dropped 8% in a single day when Amazon announced they would be lowering Whole Foods prices and moving away from their old "Whole Paycheck" pricing. And in early 2018, Amazon announced free 2-hour Whole Foods delivery in certain markets.

Amazon's strategy goes far beyond creating operational efficiencies. Nearly 100 million Americans, probably including you, are Amazon Prime customers, who pay $119 per year for free shipping, plus a host of no-additional-cost benefits like streaming video on demand. The goal, of course, is to "lock" those customers into always buying from Amazon, thus taking business from Walmart, Target, and similar competitors.

And Amazon is working to harness technology to change the very nature of delivering products. Plenty of people are scoffing at the notion of delivery-by-drone . . . but don't be surprised how fast the world changes if Amazon really makes it possible! And you can already shop at Amazon Go locations where your smartphone tracks your purchases, which avoids waiting in line to check out while someone in front of you pays with a check!

Companies like Uber and Amazon have disrupted entire industries with new business models, economies of scale, and ruthless pricing. You're not immune from those threats.

John's Note: I like to ask accountants that believe what they do is too complicated for a computer or a robot if they think Amazon will be delivering by drone to their door by 2030, they all concede that it is likely. I then ask, "you think the technology for a drone, connected to GPS and reading its environment so it does not run into other drones and has to deal with birds and a myriad of other obstacles to deliver a package from a warehouse to your, not your neighbors, front door, is less complicated than putting numbers in boxes"?

But there are even bigger dangers to your practice, and they come from machine learning and artificial intelligence.

JOB	ODDS OF DOOM
Tax Preparer	99%
Accountant	94%
Financial Advisor	58%

SOURCE: WillRobotsTakeMyJob.com

Check out a scary website at WillRobotsTakeMyJob.com. It's easy to navigate. All you have to do is enter your job title, then click to see the odds that it will be computerized. (The site takes its data from a 2013 Oxford University report.)

We'll start with the accountants. Everyone knows what they do, right? Bookkeeping and payroll services for smaller businesses, audits and attestations for bigger firms, and business and personal tax prep for everyone. Let's call this traditional breed of practitioner "CPA 1.0" for short.

The fundamental problem with these services is that developing technology has made it too easy for clients to do it themselves. And that technology is making it easier and easier all the time.

Decades ago, accountants kept books in handwritten ledgers and calculated numbers by hand. Then they moved to spreadsheets and ten-keys. Now it's QuickBooks® and a host of cloud-based providers to automate those vital processes. And as those programs advanced, smart marketers got the bright idea to cut out the middleman and market them directly to end-users (otherwise known as "your clients").

We all know that giving the average business owner a copy of QuickBooks® and telling him to go knock himself out is like giving an average suburban mom a bone saw and wishing her luck with her kids' broken arm. But that doesn't matter. What matters is how the companies who sell those programs create the perception, in their millions of buyers' minds, that they really can "do it themselves."

Telling clients how much they made, how much they're worth, and how much they owe the government is important stuff. CPAs have ridden that horse for decades. In the process, they've established a reputation for integrity and made themselves the most trusted financial advisors of all. If you're not one yourself, you'd be perfectly happy if your daughter brought one home to marry.

If you're a traditional accountant, focusing your practice on payroll, bookkeeping and tax prep, you're an endangered species. You know this, right? Technological change is turning your core businesses into commodities–cheap and indistinguishable, like soap or toilet paper. And there's nothing you can do to stop the wheels of that particular progress.

John's Note: There are ways to brand a commodity product. A t-shirt (commodity) with a swoosh (brand) on it will cost more than a plain t-shirt. (My wife insists that the "Egglands Best" is a better egg, and I'm not going to tell her it's just an egg).

But you'll note that the companies that succeed in branding commodity products have generally improved the products as well, such as with higher-quality fabrics, and created unique designs that customers can't get with commodities. So, yes, it's possible to carve out a niche within a commodity–but it's not easy, as the shirt and egg examples illustrate.

TurboTax® has a phone app that lets a user snap a photo of their W2 and turn it into a 1040-EZ. Yes, we know these users aren't your clients–but this sort of technology will only get better over time. It will make its way to clients further up the financial food chain. And that will only make your tax-prep services less valuable.

It used to be that developing technology helped you do your job more efficiently. Now, artificial intelligence and machine learning are poised to do it for you. If your business, your income, and your financial security are based on recording history for your clients, you should be very, very afraid.

Artificial intelligence and machine learning don't pose quite the same risk to financial advisors as they do to accountants. That's because their business isn't quite as dependent on routine tasks like an accountant's. Financial advisors typically have a smaller number of higher-value clients than an accountant generating the same revenue, which suggests there's a higher value to those relationships. (If you're an accountant considering adding financial services, take note!)

Technology has already made it a snap for clients to buy life insurance and investments on their own. Just click any of the online insurance marketplaces and they'll find hundreds of life insurance alternatives. Open an account at Schwab, Fidelity, or TD/Ameritrade and they'll find low commissions, access to the same packaged products, and even the same investment research they might get from you.

> *John's Note: For financial advisors who think they are immune, how many of you offer term life quotes? This used to be big business and a regular part of a good practice. But downward pressure on commissions and web services have largely made this something very few advisors bother with. This model will spread to other parts of the business.*

We all know that giving the average investor an E*Trade account and letting them loose on the markets is about as likely to succeed as giving the average business owner that copy of QuickBooks® we talked about. You can give an investor all the charting software, market "heatmaps," and mutual fund star ratings in the world, and it won't guarantee success. The best tools in the world are useless (or worse!) if they're used in the wrong hands.

But clients don't see it that way, and their perception is our reality. We live in a world where "answers" are just a Google search away. Some clients who have Amazon Alexa or Google Home don't even have to open their computer! They just ask, "Alexa, where should I invest my money today?" and they'll get instant "wisdom" from the all-hearing, all-knowing device on the kitchen counter.

Many advisors have used asset allocation as their first line of defense against the online brokers. They trot out the oft-quoted 1986 Brinson, Hood, and Beebower study finding that asset allocation explains 93.6% of investment returns, and argue that clients need an experienced advisor to allocate their portfolio to the right asset-class buckets. (Never mind that the study actually said that asset allocation explains 93.6% of the variability in investment returns.)

Of course, it didn't take long for the online brokers to add asset-allocation calculators to their sites. (Google it, and you'll find almost half a million results.)

Oh, and financial pornographers would have clients believe that magazines are all they need. Why pay an advisor 1% of assets under management when you can get one year (12 months) of Money magazine for $14.95? That would be great if knowing "12 Hot Funds to Buy Right Now" were the key to retiring in style. (Unfortunately for those naïve readers, it's not.)

John's Note: We've developed a product that deconstructs the myths that Ed is outlining with free and low-cost online services, so that we can show we have value in the portfolio design and management. Interesting that in financial services, "investment pornographers" are trying to turn something that isn't a commodity into one. That's a problem accountants don't face—yet.

Now there's a new breed of online money manager that promises to eat even more of your lunch. We're talking, of course, about dreaded robo-advisors. The most sophisticated of these programs feature fully-automated investments, self-learning algorithms, and automated asset shifts to react to changing markets and client needs. Collectively, robo-advisors managed $19 billion at the end of 2014. But that figure is expected to grow to $250 billion by 2021. And they do it for a mere fraction of the 1% fee that the typical advisor charges to keep their business going.

The bottom line here is inevitable. You can see it coming even if you don't know when it'll arrive. Insurance, per se, is just a product. Money management has become a commodity. If you want your practice to thrive, you need to give your clients more. And even if you're winding down your career, technology is attacking the equity you've built in your business like termites undermine the floor of a house. In both cases, you don't want to be there when the floor collapses!

Change is unavoidable in business. The real challenge lies in how you handle it. A century ago, buggy-whip makers reinvented themselves as leather-goods manufacturers, or they went out of business. Icemakers reinvented themselves as refrigeration specialists, or they went bankrupt.

If you're in the business of managing money or selling financial products—and nothing more—your business isn't just threatened. Your business is broken.

So how will you reinvent yourself?

Here's the Solution

So, what's the solution? For accountants, it's moving away from compliance services and towards advisory services. For financial advisors, it's giving yourself an added-value edge that clients can't get from providers based around technology platforms.

And for both groups, it starts with taxes. Taxes are the tip of the spear that drives client engagement. If you don't get the taxes right, nothing else matters.

We say you should kick off any client engagement with a formal tax plan that includes a tangible deliverable. It's a high-value service that takes you well outside the role of recording history that occupies most accountants and tax preparers and the commodity products and investment-management that occupy most financial advisors. It's a high-touch service that relies on

FORMAL PROACTIVE PLANNING

Every tax preparer, and most financial advisors, has done at least some informal tax planning for their clients. You sit down with a client to a 1040 or life insurance policy, and the client moans about

the check they have to write to the IRS. You recommend something smart, and appropriate, and realistic for the client. The client smiles and thanks you for what really is valuable advice. You pat yourself on the back and congratulate yourself for adding value through your proactive planning service.

Here's the problem with that sort of verbal, ad hoc planning. Clients don't do anything with it! They forget half of what you told them by the time they get out to their car, and the rest by the time they get home. A year later, they come back to your office, and you see they've repeated the same mistakes and missed the same opportunities all over again!

- The solution here–and this is the foundation of the entire Tax Master Network®–is to give clients a written plan–a tangible deliverable the client can literally hold onto to remind them what to do and who told them to do it. Seems archaic in a digital world, but the tangible is still the most powerful tool.

- One of our Tax Master Network® members tells a great story about how he solved this issue for a client. The client was a roofing contractor, operating his business as a sole proprietor, and making over $100,000 a year. Our member saw that his client was paying more self-employment tax than he had to. So he told the client to form an S corp. He spent 20 minutes explaining how it worked and how to establish it. Naturally, the client thanked him and said he would get right on it.

- Fast forward one year. The client shows up at our member's office for his tax return and, sure enough, there's no S corp. So that year, our member did things a little different. He sold the client a formal tax plan. And what do you think he recommended the client do first? Form an S corp, of course!

- This time the results were different. This time the client had actual skin in the game! This time the client acted on our member's advice. This time, the client got the benefit of the savings our member had proposed.

- Think about this for a minute. The client got more value from paying for planning than he did from all that "free advice" that, in the end, didn't save him a dime.

- Ultimately, free advice is worth what your client pays for it. Verbal advice is worth the paper it's printed on. This is especially true for complex issues like taxes. The solution to both these problems is formal planning that leads to a tangible deliverable.

What should that formal planning process look like? Here's an easy-to-explain analogy that uses a model all of your clients should immediately understand.

DIAGNOSE   PRESCRIBE   FILL

What happens when you go to the doctor? Usually three specific things, in specific order:

1. The process starts with a diagnosis. Does your stomach hurt? What could it be? Did you get some bad blue cheese in your salad last night? Maybe it's just mild food poisoning. Is there acute upper abdominal pain? Maybe it's pancreatitis. Have you felt bad for weeks or months? Uh oh . . . maybe it's contagious death cancer, and it's time to start getting your affairs in order.

1. Next, the doctor prescribes a solution. This could involve a visit to a specialist, medication, surgery, physical therapy, or any combination of the above.

2. Finally, someone fills the prescription–a pharmacist, a surgeon, a therapist, or someone else. (Note that it's often someone else who fills that prescription–this will be important, especially for financial advisors, when you bring in outside experts to implement the parts of the plan that are outside your expertise.)

The table below outlines some examples of diagnosing, prescribing, and filling prescriptions. You'll see it's an easy way to explain almost any tax strategy and help your clients understand how your new service can
help them.

DIAGNOSE	PRESCRIBE	FILL
Too much SE tax?	Establish S-corp	• File paper • Obtain EIN • Make S election
Missed medical deductions	Establish MERP	• Fill out plan • Track expenses • Reimburse expenses
Missed depreciation?	Cost Segregation	• Hire vendor • Schedule study • File Form 3115

So, now we've outlined a better model for a formal tax planning service. It's an advisory service, not a compliance service, which means it's poised to survive the coming technological change about to sweep through the accounting and financial industries. And it's a high-value service, that can't be replaced by an online portal or platform, that positions you as a hero in your clients' eyes. Now let's talk about how to start selling it.

John's Note: If you are thinking the "filling" portion looks like a lot of work, it is, unless you have an online pharmacy where you can place the orders for your client.

How to Build Your Tax Planning Business

> "If you get up early, work late, and pay your taxes, you will get rich – if you strike oil."
>
> J. Paul Getty

Now that we've defined exactly what we mean by formal, proactive tax planning, let's talk about how to start building your business. The process involves three steps: 1) identify appropriate prospects; 2) craft a winning marketing message; and 3) close client engagements. (Those of you who became accountants so you wouldn't have to "close sales," don't panic–if you do the first steps right, you won't have to push to close sales at all.)

> *John's Note: If I buy milk at the grocery store, it could be said the grocery store "closed" the milk sale. But, I had cereal, I needed milk, I bought it. Ed will teach you to provide the cereal. Buying the milk is just a natural reaction to having cereal, no selling necessary!*

Prospecting for Tax Savings

The process starts with identifying suspects–people who are in pain or could be in pain over their taxes.

There are plenty of people who will be happy to tell you they're in pain over their tax bill right now. These people are obvious suspects. And there are plenty more who are paying more tax than they need to, but don't realize it or don't feel pain over it yet. These people can be suspects, too. You just have to work a little harder getting them to realize it or feel the pain.

Where do you find them? On Facebook? LinkedIn? Twitter? Advertising in the local business section? What about the local Chamber of Commerce? In most cases, you should start a lot closer to home. Take a look at what we call the "concentric circle" theory of prospecting and see.

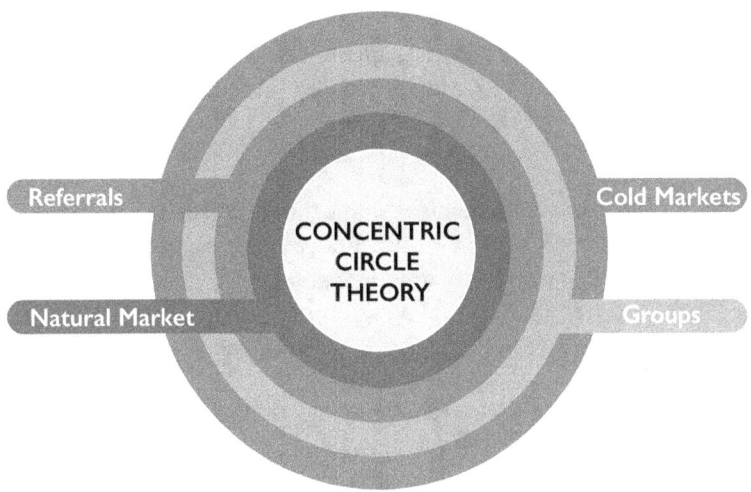

Natural Markets

It's a truism that people want to do business with people they know, they like, and they trust. That sounds like a pretty tall order, finding enough of them to launch a business. But most of us already have a sizable group of people who know us, like, us and trust us. They're called our "natural market," and you'll find them at the very center of the circle. These are the first people we talk to when we launch our new business. They're the people who come to us simply because we're in business now. (If you're in the life insurance business, they're the people you included in your "Project 100" and "Business 100" booklets you put together while you were getting licensed.

Now, some people (the "lucky sperm club") have enough prospects in their natural market to build an entire business around. If you grew up in Palm Beach and you want to broker yachts, or your last name is "Rockefeller," and you want to sell art, you're probably in good shape. But most of us aren't that lucky . . . we have to work a little harder to expand our "marketing funnel" to be sure we draw in enough clients to succeed.

Don't take your natural market for granted. If you're a CPA, opening a new practice, there may be clients who come to you simply because it's you offering those services. But it's still important to let them know how you're different from other CPAs and more valuable. When it comes time to ask them for referrals, do you want them to tout you because you're their sister's nephew, or because you saved them $6,000 that their old CPA missed?

Referrals

Take another look at the circle. What's the next step out from the natural market? Referrals. For most of you, this should be the most important word in marketing your business. Not Facebook. Not "social media." Not funnels. Not pay-per-click, or direct mail, or any of the other shiny tools that vendors will tempt you with. Referrals.

Why are referrals so valuable? Because, while they may not know you, like you, or trust you now, they have direct personal connections to the people who already do. And that makes them easier and faster to close than any other kind of prospect you don't already know.

Referrals are also generally less likely to quibble over fees. If you're expensive–and you should be–referrals already know that! And in an odd psychological twist, they're probably reluctant to let the client who referred them to you see them quibbling over fees.

Finally, clients who come to you via referral are more likely to give you more referrals themselves. That's because they're more comfortable with the referral process. They understand the value of referrals. They understand how that process works. And they're less likely to perceive any risk in the process than a client who isn't used to it.

Groups

Take another look at the circle. The next step out is the groups that your clients belong to. If you target a particular market, it's likely that they belong to some sort of group or groups . . . and you can target attention on those groups to find more of those clients.

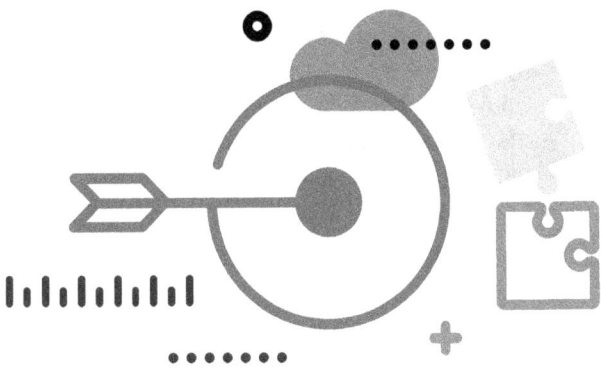

Here are some of the reasons target marketing is so effective, especially with specific professional groups:

1. You'll come to learn your target market's specific challenges and concerns. As we'll discuss later in this chapter, clients generally make the decision to buy with their emotions, then look for logic and reason to back up those emotions. If you understand what drives those emotions, especially the sources of their pain and frustration, you'll have a powerful reason for them to come to you for help with their problems.

2. You'll get to learn and speak your target market's individual language. Speaking a group's language is a little-known and subtle but powerful strategy for bonding, building rapport, and getting them to know you, like you, and trust you.

   • Let's say you're targeting real estate agents, and you come to them with three distinct service packages. Most of us are familiar with "Silver," "Gold," and "Platinum" levels. (My favorite marketing guru manages a top-level "Titanium" level–how does he top that?)

   • Now, there's nothing wrong with silver, gold, and platinum–there are entire stores at every mall in America dedicated to selling them. But what if you could tailor your packages to something that resonates more effectively with your market?

   • As it turns out, real estate agents generally distinguish

between three markets of buyers. There's the "starter" home buyer, looking for their first home. (Never mind that in pricey areas like San Francisco, a "starter" home goes for a million dollars or more.) There's the "move-up" buyer, who's ready for something more. And there's the "executive" buyer, who wants to reward himself with something more showy and substantial.

- You've probably already figured out where we're going here. Why target real estate agents with silver, gold, and platinum when you can target them with more-relevant starter, move-up, and executive packages. You'll even get to put a little psychology to work for yourself . . . who wants to tell their friends they just signed up for the starter package?

3. You can build a reputation as your target market's "go to" provider for whatever services you offer. It's one thing to be, for example, a CPA who works with real estate agents. It's another thing entirely to be the CPA who specializes in working with them–especially if you have enthusiastic clients who are happy to refer you to their colleagues. Remember "know . . . like . . . trust." If you build a reputation within your target market's groups, you'll climb that.

SEMINARS THAT **SELL**

Do you like giving seminars? Great! So do we! Seminars let you leverage your time by speaking to groups instead of individuals. That's an immediate plus.

But seminars create a powerful psychological edge in an audience's mind, compared to one-on-one meetings. Simply put, in a seminar setting, you get to position yourself as a teacher rather than a salesman.

4. Nobody likes to be "sold." Play a word association game and ask ten people to tell you the first thing they think of when you mention the word "salesman" Easily eight or nine of them will reply with "used cars." Think of a movie about salespeople, and most people turn to the high-pressure boiler room from *Glengarry Glen Ross*. ("Third prize is you're fired.")

That's a shame. Sales is an honorable profession and an absolutely necessary engine of our economy–nothing happens until someone decides to buy. But it's not going out on a limb to say that "selling" is a negative term for a lot of people.

Here's how seminars help sidestep that perception problem. When prospects perceive that you're trying to sell them something, their defenses go up. But when they perceive you're trying to teach them something, they don't get so defensive.

This is even truer if some sort of group, like a trade group or professional association, brings you in as an invited guest (as opposed to the traditional financial advisor seminar where you send out 3,000 invitations to get a couple of dozen prospects to a dinner at a steakhouse). The easiest and best way to assemble an audience for a seminar is definitely to have someone else do it on your behalf. That way, the group's credibility and endorsement will rub off on you, and this "teacher versus salesman" benefit will be even stronger.

The key to making the most of any seminar is absolute clarity of purpose. What, exactly, are you trying to do with your time in front of the group? (Hint: it's probably not what you think it should be.) There are three things you can do with any audience, whether you assemble it yourself or take advantage of an invitation to speak:

1. You can educate them. This is probably what you think

should be your primary goal . . . but it's not. Yes, educating your audience is important. If you don't give them good information in exchange for the time they spend with you, they'll feel ripped-off and resentful. But as we'll see with Reason #3, you're not there to teach them how to do whatever it is you want to do for them.

- You're not teaching a CE class, and it's a mistake to focus on technical details. And honestly, most audiences forget half of what you say by the end of the day and the rest by the end of the week anyway.

2. **You can entertain them.** This is probably more important than you think. Remember, people want to buy from people they know, they like, and they trust. If you bore them, they won't like you, and they won't pay attention to you. This means they won't learn anything.

- The good news is, entertaining an audience–especially when the topic is taxes–is a lot easier than you might think. You don't have to dazzle them with Stephen Colbert quips or Jimmy Fallon one-liners. Just tell a couple of dad jokes and let your personality show through, and you'll be just fine. (If you're truly humor-challenged, the Tax Master Network® seminar presentation scripts include enough entertaining comments and observations that you won't have worry about adding any of your own.)

3. **You can motivate them.** This is the key. This is the real goal of most seminars. You can stand in front of an audience for an hour and dazzle them with your knowledge. You can make them laugh or make them cry. But in the end, if they don't do anything with the information you give them, you may as well do a juggling act, sing a couple of songs, or do some card tricks. What good is the education you give them if you don't motivate them to do something with it?

- In most cases, your goal will be quite clear. You'll want your audience to sign up for a "Tax Assessment" (Financial Gravity's term), or Tax Analysis, or Tax Appraisal (if you're working with real estate audiences), or Tax MRI (if you're working with doctors), or whatever else you call your initial appointment. (Whatever you do, don't call it a "free consultation." That's what everyone else offers, and it tells prospects they get to sit down and pick your brain for free for 60 minutes, with no obligation to reward you for that time with any future business.)

Cold Markets

Take a final look at the concentric circles. What's the final ring? The one orbiting somewhere out there beyond Pluto? That's right, totally cold markets. People who don't know you, don't like you and don't trust you. At least, not yet. Maybe someday. But it's going to take a lot more time and effort to get them there than it will for anyone in the natural market, referral, and group circles.

Why would you want to target people who don't know you from Adam unless and until you've exhausted all the warmer markets inside that outermost ring?

If you must try cold marketing, we generally recommend with social media. It's inexpensive to start and easy to test. Facebook, especially, feels like a safe space for most users. Yes, advertising on Facebook is still advertising. But it's surrounded by graduation photos, vacation snapshots, and cute kittens and puppies. Something about the setting seems to pull your message closer to the center of the concentric circles and feel less cold.

Craft a Compelling Message

Here's the biggest problem with selling most financial services. Nobody really wants them. Seriously, think about it. Who wakes up in the morning, refreshed after a great night's sleep, and springs out of bed to say "today is the day I'm going to hire a great accountant!" Nobody, that's who. And while clients look forward to "liquidity events" like selling a business or retiring with a seven-figure retirement nest egg, nobody looks forward to the challenge of trying to distinguish one wealth manager from another.

- Payroll/Accounting Services
- Tax Prep
- Insurance
- Investment/Wealth Management
- Tax Savings
- Dollars at a Discount

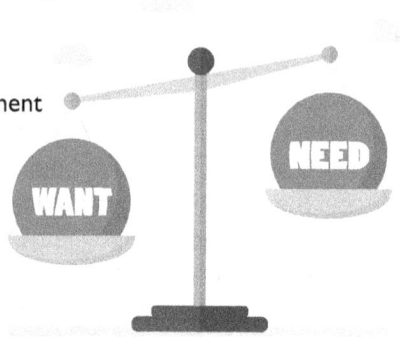

That's where the need to craft a compelling marketing message is so important. We all know it's easier to sell people something they want than it is to sell them something they need. So how do you transform a humdrum commodity service into something they get excited about?

Payroll processing has long been a mainstay of many accounting firms. It's also a really crappy business to be in. Clients just don't appreciate it. You get it right, or you screw it up, but there's never a chance to be a hero. Steady income, yes, but low fees, all down-side, and no upside. And technology is squeezing margins harder here than anywhere else in your business. At this point, most Tax Master Network® members just outsource it to one of the national giants in exchange for a steady commission with no liability. They've concluded it's just not worth the hassle any other way . . . and their clients don't care that it's outsourced.

Basic accounting services aren't much better. Clients understand, grudgingly, that accurate books and records are "important." But few business owners get excited about putting in the work that's necessary to make that happen. (If they liked it, they'd be keeping their own books, or even competing with you!) But again, you screw them up, or you get them "right"–the balance sheets balance and the debits match the credits. There's not much opportunity to be a hero with bookkeeping. This is the "recording history" trap we talked about in the first chapter. And, like payroll processing, basic bookkeeping is pretty much doomed in an era of machine learning and artificial intelligence.

Tax prep is the next rung of the financial service ladder. Like payroll processing and basic bookkeeping, it's something clients pay for because they need to, not because they want to. But unlike those services, tax prep gives you a fighting chance to be a hero. You can help clients find deductions they would have missed on their own. And you can spot opportunities to pivot from **tax prep** to **tax planning.**

At the same time, the tax prep business faces real pressures that will make it far less valuable in the coming years. More and more clients are becoming comfortable with "accountant in a box" software that lets them do it themselves. (Some of those programs even let them submit their return to a real accountant for review before filing!) The Tax Cuts and Jobs Act of 2017 will cut the number of itemizers in half, which will convince more clients to take the plunge and switch to software. More and more car dealers are offering tax-prep services to convert refunds into down payments! And, as with payroll and bookkeeping, artificial intelligence and machine learning will make the whole process easier, pushing fees down.

(At this point, we should make a brief note for financial advisors. Many of you have added "$49 tax preparation" or "$99 tax preparation" services to your practice, not because you think it's a great revenue source, but because you think it's a great prospecting funnel. And it may be, if you're looking for cheapskate price shoppers with bank CDs that you can move to annuities. But that's no way to attract affluent business owners with six-figure and seven-figure portfolios. You know what is a good way to attract them? Planning, that's what! Ditch the cheap tax-prep clients, focus on high-income, high-value planning prospects, and you'll probably be a lot happier.)

John's Note: I built the $49 tax business thinking it was a great loss leader. It gave me lots of headaches, and three years in I could see that it wasn't leading to anything I wanted. The real loss I suffered was the thickness and pigment of my hair.

Switching over to the financial services side, we'll start with insurance. Most people need it. But nobody wants it. That's why it's hard to sell, even when it can solve so many problems. (Lots of fans say that permanent life insurance is the "Swiss army knife" of financial products. They're not wrong.)

Having said that, most substantial life insurance policies aren't sold just for death benefits that clients need. They're sold for tax-planning advantages that clients want: tax-advantaged retirement income, tax-advantaged charitable planning, tax-motivated estate planning, and the like. If you specialize in those sorts of markets, you're already in the tax business. So why not add comprehensive, holistic tax planning to uncover more insurance prospects and deliver more ideas, savings, and value to the clients you close?

Finally, there's the big umbrella of "financial services." Whether you focus on the planning side or the asset management side, you're at least selling something clients want. But you're also selling something they can buy almost anywhere: at the bank, in a fancy downtown office, in suburban offices, and online. As much as clients want the financial success and security and peace of mind you're selling, you need something to stand out from the crowd so they buy it from you.

That, of course, is where tax planning comes in. Clients hate paying taxes. They *want* to pay less. So why not show them how to do it, in ways that funnel them into whatever business you're in? Want accounting clients? Tax savings are the best way to get them in the door. Want insurance prospects? Tax savings are the best way to get them in the door. Want more assets to manage? Tax savings are the best way to gather them!

HOW CLIENTS **DECIDE**

Now that we've identified tax planning as something clients really want, let's talk a little bit about the psychology involved in buying it. You may not think "psychology" plays much part in buying mundane services like accounting and financial management. But those readers–especially the accountants–who have never been through a sales training course might be surprised just how powerful a little bit of understanding can be. (No, the lame "marketing" classes your professional association sponsors for free CE credit don't count.)

If you've ever taken an economics class, you probably spent the first day listening to your professor introduce you to homo economicus, or "rational man." Homo economicus is a smart fellow who looks at financial decisions with a rational eye, evaluates the costs and benefits of different options, and makes the rational decision to maximize his benefit. If you needed financial advice, homo economicus is the guy you'd turn to yourself.

There's just one problem. Homo economicus doesn't exist! People aren't rational. People are emotional. And there's an entirely new branch of economics, called behavioral economics or behavioral finance, that exists to understand and harness how real-world people use emotions to make right choices and wrong choices every day. (Don't take our word for it. Just look at the lineup of Nobel Prize winners and see how many behavioral economists appear on that list.)

> *John's Note: There are a bunch of great books on this topic that will help you make smarter choices and work more effectively with clients. Start with Daniel Ariely's, Predictably Irrational. He has two follow-up books as well. Then, when Amazon sees you bought these you will get inundated with the vast world of behavioral economics.*

Specifically, what motivates clients to buy? The answer, in short, is emotion, not logic. And which emotions drive decisions? Well, Wall Street runs on two engines: greed and fear. Pain and gain. And it turns out pain is by far the stronger motivator. In fact, behavioral economists have determined that people feel the emotional impact of pain twice as strongly as they feel the emotional impact of gain. They even have a name for the phenomenon. It's called "loss aversion," and it's one of the dozens of heuristics (cognitive shortcuts) that behavioral economists have identified that drive consumer and investor decision making.

PAIN VS GAIN

What does this tell us when it comes to selling tax savings? It tells us to focus on the emotional *pain* of paying too much tax, rather than the potential *gain* of paying less.

Let's say you've delivered a terrific seminar presentation to a group of local business owners. One comes in for their free Tax Assessment, and you discover he's overpaying his taxes by $5,000 per year. Which of these two statements do you think will get him more emotionally invested in solving that problem?

A. "Wow! Based on the information you've just given me, I can save you $5,000 per year in taxes!"

• Or . . .

B. Wow! Based on the information you've just given me, you're wasting $5,000 per year in taxes you don't have to pay!"

On paper, both of those statements should be equally effective. *Homo economicus* would look and see the same $5,000 both times, and conclude they're the same. But trust us, and trust your own common sense, when we tell you that prospects will act far faster and more decisively to stop wasting $5,000 per year than they ever will to secure a new $5,000 in gain.

This specific scenario illustrates a second behavioral finance heuristic called the "endowment effect." People feel much more strongly about something they have (say, a bird in the hand) than they do about something they don't have now but might have in the future (like, say, two in the bush). So focus on the $5,000 that they already have and help them feel the emotional impact of knowing they're wasting it. You'll find it far more effective than dangling the chance to save $5,000 they never had in the first place.

Many of the Tax Master Network® marketing strategies are built around bringing out this pain. Our business owner seminar kit, for example, is built around "10 Most Expensive Tax Mistakes," not "10 Most Valuable Tax Savings Opportunities." That's because we've split-tested it with different audiences, and "Mistakes" sells more appointments than "Opportunities."

The Elevator Speech

Let's finish this discussion with a quick look at the fastest way to open a conversation with someone who might have an interest in your service. We're talking, of course, about the elevator speech. The key here is to forget about the initial after your name–no matter how important they are to you–and focus on what you do.

THE ELEVATOR SPEECH

Go to a cocktail party, or your kid's ball game, or a neighborhood barbecue, and tell people you're a CPA, and they might wonder what kind of CPA you are–auditor, tax pro, consultant, or controller–but they probably won't care much beyond that. Tell them you're an enrolled agent, and you've at least narrowed it down to the "tax" arena–assuming, of course, they even know what an EA is–but again, they won't get very excited about it. Tell them you're a financial advisor, and they'll immediately bring their own assumptions and prejudices to the conversation or probably excuse themselves from the conversation entirely.

But if you tell them what you **do** and not what you **are,** it's a different story. Tell them, "I help business owners stop overpaying their taxes," and you'll attract some attention. You might even start a conversation that leads to some business. And you'll certainly make a better impression than if you just say, "I'm a CPA."

We all realize that letters like "CPA," "EA," and "CFP" represent a lot of work. They represent good things like integrity, accountability, and attention to detail. They're the most trusted letters in all of financial services.

But few people besides us realize all that–and even if they do, they're not likely to care. They want to know what's in it for them.

So don't tell people you're a CPA, or an EA, or anything else. Don't be anything at all. Instead, do something. Do something people want done, like saving tax. You already do that! So do it well, and do it differently than anyone else. Then tell people what you do instead of what you are. We promise you'll turn a lot more questions into conversations!

> *John's Note: I open conversations by telling listeners, "I help small business owners lower their personal income taxes." I usually get, "Are you a CPA." I answer, "When was the last time you got advice from your CPA that saved you at least $1000 a year in taxes." 100% of the time, they reply NEVER. This is why CPA's need to do something to distance themselves from other CPA's! You don't want to be mixed in with the ones that aren't saving money on taxes, and if you don't distance yourselves, advisors will work to lump you into the "every other CPA" category. Advisors, this will help you drive a wedge into the "most trusted advisor" issue–when you deliver the Tax Blueprint®, that's when the CPA gets fired.*

How to Open Cases

Once you've identified a suspect, the next step is to see if you can get them interested enough to listen to your pitch and consider your offer. At that point, once they've raised their hand and said "I'm interested," they become a prospect. Your next step, in most cases, will be to close them for an actual appointment where you can go into more depth and hopefully close a plan sale.

Here's a five-step system that we recommend Tax Master Network® members use to turn suspects into bona fide prospects. It's quick and easy. It starts by piquing the listener's attention, introduces your planning service, outlines how the process works, identifies your role in the process, and even insulates you from technical questions you might not feel comfortable or capable of answering.

I. START THE CONVERSATION

"When was the last time your tax pro came to you and said, 'Here's an idea I think will save you money?"

Step one is to start the conversation in a way that engages your listener and draws them in. As with the elevator speech, you can't just tell them who you are or even what you do and expect them to care. You have to grab their interest by telling them what value you deliver.

Here at Tax Master Network®, we recommend what we call the Magic Question. It's straightforward, simple, and devastatingly effective:

When was the last time
your tax pro came to you and said,
"Here's an idea I think will save you money?"

Try it yourself. You'll quickly find that the answer is almost always "never."

Ironically, most tax pros actually do give their clients plenty of ideas to save money. But it's the sort of informal, ad hoc advice we dismantled in the last chapter. There's no separate engagement, no fee, and no tangible deliverable. So the client doesn't remember that the advice was even offered, and the tax pro gets no credit for offering it.

We call this a "wedge question" because it immediately drives a wedge between your listener and their current tax pro. Merely asking the question is enough to get them thinking: "Why isn't my guy bringing me ideas? What am I missing?" Asking when was the last time it happened subtly implies that it should be happening regularly.

(Here's a business development plan for accountants that's easily worth 100 times the cost of this book. Find one new business owner per day ask them this question. I guarantee your business will grow faster than it ever has in any previous year.)

John's Note: Financial advisors, the same goes for you! First of all, it's tough to get to a business owner because they KNOW you're going to pitch them one of the three things I mentioned earlier. This is a way to unlock access to a huge untapped market. What we won't be covering in this book are the two dozen+ products and services that will make a profound impact on the business owner. But none of them open doors like tax planning. Once you're in, you can change their lives. Really, it's that big.

2. INTRODUCE YOUR OFFER

"I help (target market here) pay less tax, legally, morally, and ethically."

Now that you've got your listener's attention, it's time to introduce your offer. It couldn't be simpler: "I help people just like you to pay less tax." If you're feeling ambitious, you can tell them it's legal, moral, and ethical, too. (No harmful carbohydrates or trans fats, either!)

This statement works because it promises to deliver the value you've just helped your listener realize they aren't already getting from their current tax relationship. It also sets you apart from other tax professionals by focusing on a service that, frankly, most of them don't even offer.

3. EXPLAIN HOW IT WORKS

"It works like going to the doctor. We start with a diagnosis, prescribe a solution, then fill the prescription"

So far, you've driven a wedge between your listener and their current accountant, and you've given them the benefit of working with you. But your listener has no idea how tax planning works, in general or for them. So now you tell them, with the great diagnose/prescribe/fill analogy we discussed in the last chapter. This will lay out the process in a way they immediately understand and feel comfortable with.

4. OUTLINE YOUR ROLE

"When it comes to some areas, like (your specialty), I'll fill the prescription for you."

If your prospect likes what they hear, give them a little more detail to emphasize your area expertise. But this isn't just an opportunity for you to brag! Remember, you're introducing a whole new kind of service. The value here comes from the comprehensive approach. So do your best to subordinate your own ego to the overall value you bring.

5. PIVOT TO DISCLAIMER

"When it comes to other areas, like (what you

don't do), we'll work with (outside advisors)'"

This last step may seem obvious. Of course, you don't do every-thing, even if your organization does. But this is an important first step in training your future client and setting realistic expectations. It's especially valuable if you're worried that your technical knowl-edge in a particular area is lacking. Telling the client up front that you won't be able to answer all of their technical questions right off the top of your head is a great way to stop worrying that they might ask you a question you can't answer!

This may be especially important for financial advisors. When you start talking taxes, most people will immediately assume that you're a CPA–or that you should be one to help with taxes. That's not true, of course, as we've already seen–most CPAs don't do any formal tax planning at all! But it gives you a built-in answer for the prospect who asks, "are you a CPA?" Your answer should be, "no . . . didn't we just establish that CPAs aren't really bringing you the savings you want?" Your follow up should be that you work with accounting professionals who can actually implement the planning ideas for things like business entities that are outside your particu-lar skills.

John's Note: I was just thinking, if only there were a "done for you" marketing program that included marketing on social networks like Facebook, that drove prospects to a landing page with great content like maybe a weekly "newsletter" type thing that tied current events to tax planning. With offers for free stuff, like books and special reports, which gave you permission to talk about a litany of products and services, that improves the small business, including proactive tax planning. If only . . .

How to Close Tax Plan Sales

You've identified a suspect who you think might benefit from your new tax-planning service. You've opened the case and found that he's in pain and wants to learn more. Now it's time to close the sale! Here's a four-step system that Tax Master Network® members across the country have used to sell literally millions of dollars in tax planning fees. It's certainly not the only way to do it, and we want you to add your own twists as you see what does and doesn't work for you. But this should give you a basic framework for building out a system you can feel comfortable using over time.

It starts with scheduling an appointment. But don't call it a "consultation!" Prospects expect a "consultation" means they get to sit down and pick your brain for an hour of free advice before deciding whether they want to do business with you. But we want you in the driver's seat–so offer an "analysis" of some sort that implies the prospect will walk away with specific information at the end.

(If you're targeting a specific market like we recommended in the last section, pick a name that resonates with your market. If you're targeting doctors, for example, consider a "tax diagnosis" or "1040 MRI." If you're targeting real estate agents, consider a "tax appraisal," etc. Don't be afraid to come up with more than one name if you're targeting more than one kind of prospect!)

Let the client know exactly what to expect. "We'll sit down together with your returns, and I'll ask you a bunch of questions about your income. We'll find the mistakes and missed opportunities that could be costing you thousands of dollars in wasted taxes, then figure out what to do about it."

I. IDENTIFY MISTAKES AND MISSED OPPORTUNITIES

- Diagnosis
- Client-centered
- Hit close to home

Your goal here in this first step is a diagnosis, plain and simple, just like you get at the doctor. What mistakes is your prospect making? What savings opportunities are they missing?

You want your analysis to be client-centered. By that, we mean you want them to see that you're looking specifically at their unique situation, not just throwing out the same one-size-fits-all solution for everyone. (Remember the "hammer-nail" problem we discussed in the last chapter?) A year ago, a Florida-based tax-planning firm advertised on satellite radio that they could cut their clients' tax bills to less than 10% of their income. Now how can they do something like that before they even see those tax returns?

In the same vein, you want this step to hit close to home. Don't tell a prospect "business owners sometimes fail to take or pick the right way to deduct business miles." Tell them "it looks like you're losing big-time taking the mileage allowance instead of actual expenses." Don't tell them "some mutual funds trade more often, which means they generate higher capital gains." Tell them "wow, this fund is really socking you hard with taxes!" "We can help you reduce the "tax friction" of your mutual funds and ETFs."

Some planners like to have prospects send them tax returns to review before the meeting. Others feel comfortable examining them cold right on the spot. You'll probably feel more comfortable asking for returns up front, at least until you get some experience reviewing returns.

If you're new to this process, or you don't have a tax background, you might worry that you don't have enough technical knowledge for a proper diagnosis. That's an understandable fear, but it shouldn't discourage you from diving in. You're probably comparing yourself here against an expert tax planner with years of experience. And no, you won't spot as many issues or opportunities as they do. But that's not the right comparison.

Let's say that you sit down with a client and a return showing ten missed opportunities. Someone who's been doing this awhile might spot eight of them pretty quickly. You might spot just four. And yes, that's four less than the expert. But it's also four more than the prospect! That's the real comparison that matters. How much value can you deliver for the prospect, even as you're just getting start-ed? The answer is, probably enough to make them very happy. And if you learn two more strategies over the next year, they'll be just as excited to learn about those as the four you spotted right out the gate.

Sometimes people ask what they should do with a prospect who doesn't want to bring their tax returns to the initial meeting. The an-swer is easy: don't waste your time. Seriously, if they're not willing to share their returns, they're not a legitimate prospect in the first place. Move on.

2. QUANTIFY COST

- Estimates, not calculations
- Cumulative cost

The second step may be harder until you get some practice under your belt. And that involves quantifying the cost of those mistakes and missed opportunities. At Financial Gravity, we use a spread-sheet/program we have developed over many years, to help esti-mate those numbers. But you can do it in your head as long as you have a good grasp of fourth-grade arithmetic, or you can kick it old school with a pencil and calculator.

- How much can your prospect save by converting her sole pro-prietorship earning $120,000 into an S corp paying a $60,000 salary? (Obviously, that salary has to be "reasonable compen-sation" for the work she performs for the business.) Take the $60,000 no longer subject to employment tax, multiply it by 15%, and you have roughly $9,000 in savings.

- How much can a prospect in the 24% bracket save by moving $10,000 in nondeductible medical expenses into a medical expense reimbursement plan? Multiply $10,000 by 24% and you have roughly $2,400 in savings.

- How much can a prospect save by hiring his teenage son to help manage his rental properties? If the son can do $3,000 worth of work, take that amount and multiply it by the prospect's marginal tax rate (plus self-employment tax, if any). You honestly don't even want to be too precise here, because it can backfire on you. If you tell a prospect you can save them $8,450, they're going to remember that number. If you wind up saving them $8,200, you're still a hero–but they'll remember the difference. Better to play it safe and say you'll save them "about" $8,000. If it winds up being more, trust us. They won't mind the extra.

Please, please, please don't over think this step. (You detail-oriented CPAs know who you are!) You're not signing a return here. You're guesstimating a number to sell a plan. Remember the 80/20 rule–80% of your results come from your first 20% of effort. Remember that the perfect is the enemy of the good. And feel free to under guesstimate (if that's even a word) by a bit, just to give yourself some margin for comfort. This part will get easier with practice.

3. CONFRONT CLIENT

- Pain vs. gain
- Emotional reaction
- Don't let up!

The third step may also be hard at first, but for completely different reasons. Now you have to confront the prospect with the cost of those mistakes and missed opportunities. And you have to make it **hurt.**

Remember what we said earlier about pain versus gain? This is where it counts.

Let's say you've reviewed your prospect's return, asked some clarifying questions, and concluded that you can save them $15,000 per year. You play it safe and choose to present $12,000. Now, look at your client in horror, and say, "Wow . . . based on the information you've just given me, you're wasting $12,000 per year in tax you don't have to pay." And shut your mouth and wait for them to react.

You want them to experience pain. As we discussed earlier in this chapter, behavioral finance (science!) teaches us that pain is what will motivate them to say "yes" when you present your solution!

You want this to be an emotional reaction. Remember, prospects buy or not for emotional reasons, then look for logic to back up those emotions.

Here's a great way to take black-and-white numbers and convert them into emotional commitment. Ask the prospect what they would do with the wasted taxes you rescue. Would they put it into retirement savings? If so, what do they want to do when they're retired? Would they put it towards their kids' college fund? If so, what do the kids want to do when they get out of school? Would they blow it on a dream vacation? If so, where would they go? If they tell you "the beach," you want them to feel the sand under their toes, smell the salt air and margaritas, and hear the steel drum music in their mind!

This is the hard part, for those of us who aren't sociopaths. You don't want to let up on the pain. You can't let up on the pain. It's human nature, if you see someone in pain, to try and relieve that pain. As tax planners, we do that by telling the client "it's ok, I can fix the problem and save you the $12,000. We'll convert your proprietorship to an LLC, hire your wife to manage the rental property so we can set up a medical expense reimbursement plan, and hire your son to handle the landscaping."

You could certainly say all that. And you would probably see your prospect's blood pressure start to fall. You could relieve their pain right there on the spot.

But what did you just do? You just gave away the plan! Now that the prospect has no pain, what incentive do they have to buy from you? Now that you just gave away the strategies, how much will the prospect be willing to pay for them?

Don't. Let. Up. Not until the prospect says "yes" or "no" to your service. (And if they say "no," what obligation do you have to relieve their pain by revealing your strategies? Spoiler alert: none.)

Imagine roasting your prospect on a spit over an open flame. Turn the spit to find where it hurts the most. And keep it there!

4. OFFER TAX-PLANNING SOLUTION

- Plan as prescription
- Identify value
- Frame price in relation to value
- Don't give it away!

Ok. You've found a bunch of mistakes and missed opportunities that are costing your prospect thousands in taxes they don't have to pay. You've estimated the cost of those mistakes and missed opportunities, roughly, without giving in to the temptation to over-think it and quantify it to the nearest penny. (You perfectionists know who you are!) You've confronted the prospect with the cost of those mistakes and missed opportunities. Now it's time show them the path out of that pain, by selling your service as the prescription for the pain you've just uncovered!

Make sure the prospect understands exactly how much your prescription is worth. (In this case, it sounds like $12,000 per year, right?)

We'll talk about pricing models and methodologies in a bit. But be sure to frame your price in relation to the value you're deliv-ering. If you identify $12,000 per year in savings – $60,000 over the next five years – a $3,000 or $5,000 fee should sound pretty cheap in comparison. This takes advantage of yet another behav-ioral economics concept called "anchoring," which says that the first number a prospect hears–in this case, the $12,000 annual savings–will serve as the anchor against which they'll evaluate all other numbers.

Finally–and this may be another challenge until you get some prac-tice–as much as possible, don't give it away. If the prospect asks "how will you save all that money?" tell them you're not sure yet and you'll have to prepare the plan to know how. If she asks "are you talking about an S corporation?" tell her "part of your problem is that you're paying a ton of self-employment tax–an S corporation is one solution to that problem, but it's not the only one, so I'll have to do the plan to see what works best."

Ultimately, closing sales is a numbers game. You won't close them all. (In fact, if you do close them all, you're not reaching hard enough.) Remember, a baseball player who hits the ball just three out of ten at-bats makes the All-Star team. A player who hits .350 is a shoe-in for Cooperstown. Even the utility infielder hitting .223 makes a million bucks a year! You'll have no problem beating those averages. You just have to get in the game!

How to Fire the Old Accountant

Even if all goes well, there might still be just one last challenge facing you: convincing the client to fire their old accountant.

In some cases, it's easy. Tell your prospect they're wasting $10,000 or $15,000 in taxes they don't have to pay, and some of them will be more than happy to ask for their file back.

Other prospects feel like they're stuck with their current provider. If the prospect's tax pro is also their brother-in-law or their college roommate, that's a pretty high bar to clear. It may be impossibly high. Don't fret. Move on. There are plenty of prospects in the world who aren't so wedded to their current tax pro. The time you spend courting a prospect before you learn this inconvenient news is a sunk cost. Wasting more time on them won't bring the old time back.

Ideally, of course, you'll uncover this before you ask for the sale. If the prospect tells you up front that they spent four years getting drunk with their CPA at good old Tappa Kegga Brew, you can ask them up front if they're willing to switch, or at least decide whether they're likely enough to do so to justify pursuing them.

But even prospects without a special bond to their tax pro can have a hard time switching to a new professional. And there's a special psychology behind it that you should understand.

Here's the problem. When you tell a prospect they've got the wrong tax pro, you're (very subtly) suggesting they made a mistake in choosing them in the first place. And nobody likes to be told they made a mistake–it makes people defensive to hear that sort of criticism. So their shields go up, and they wind up resisting your offer.

Here's a tested line that helps separate clients from their current relationship without manipulating them or suggesting they made a mistake in the first place:

"It sounds like you've outgrown your old accountant."

Isn't that easy? You didn't pick the wrong accountant at all. In fact, they might have been perfect for where you were when you made that choice. But things have changed (and everyone knows that things change over time), and they aren't right for you now. It's not even because the old accountant has done something wrong (by missing all the tax-saving opportunities you've just found). It's because the prospect has done something right, by growing to the point where their needs are more than the old accountant can meet.

Some clients will actually let you prepare and deliver a plan before they decide to fire their old accountant–a "try before you buy" sort of move. That's fine, too. In our experience at the Tax Master Network®, once clients see what their old accountant missed, they won't want to go back anyway!

> *John's Note: It bears repeating, when you deliver the Tax Blueprint® the savings are compelling. We have more than one example of clients with family members who are CPAs, and once the client saw the plan, they would tell us "I like my (family member), but I could have paid cash for a lake house with all these savings. I'll fire him and take him to the lake house."*

How to Sell Current Clients

Now let's talk about selling tax-planning services to current clients. This is actually easier than selling to someone new–assuming, of course, that your current clients already know you, like you, and trust you. That's because you can leverage that existing relationship to tell them what new value you're going to deliver to them rather than having to sell them on something they aren't already asking for.

The difference, of course, is that you'll do it without the pain we've discussed for the last 15 pages! Now you really do want to focus on new savings, rather than

The conversation doesn't have to take long. It might sound something like this:

"Mr. Client, I want to thank you for the chance to handle your tax business over the past few years. I've enjoyed working with you, and I'm proud of the work that I've done.

Over the past (however many) years, I've focused my effort on compliance. But now I'm looking to do more. I don't want to just help you record history and tell you what you owe. I want to help you pay less … maybe a lot less. The way to do that is through formal tax planning.

So now I'm recommending we do a comprehensive tax plan. We'll take a fresh look at every aspect of your income and your expenses. We'll see where we can restructure your business, your retirement plan, and your investment portfolio to create new savings.

The fee for the service is $x,xxx. And I know you don't want to pay $x,xxx. But it's tax-deductible, of course, (assuming you're planning for the client's business). And I guarantee you'll save at least twice the fee in the first year alone, or I'll give you a complete refund.

All I need is your signature on this engagement letter, and a check or credit card authorization, and we can get started. The sooner we get started, the sooner you can start saving."

You don't have to offer a money-back guarantee, of course. But we strongly recommend you do. Most of your clients will be buying tax-planning services for the very first time. They don't know exactly what to expect, and they're taking a financial risk by paying you. So take away that risk. Reverse it, by putting it on yourself.

Our Tax Master Network® members have been using some variation of this guarantee for years, and most have never had to refund a single fee. At Financial Gravity, we guarantee clients they'll save twice their fee in the first year. (We tested a three-times-your-fee guarantee, but it didn't sell nearly as well. We suspect that prospects just thought it was too good to be true!)

At this point, we know what you're thinking. So we'll just say it. What if your client comes back and says "why haven't you been doing all of this for me already?"

The answer lies in the difference between ad hoc tax planning and formal tax planning that we discussed in the first chapter.

"Well, like I said, I've focused my effort on compliance. And like I said, I'm proud of the work I've done. (If you've given the client any specific savings suggestions, feel free to mention them—and quantify them—here.) But we've never sat down to do this sort of formal, comprehensive planning. It's a new service that I'm just adding now, because I see the value. And I'd rather bring this to you now than not at all."

That's really all it takes. Here's the thing you have to take confidence in. Clients hate paying taxes. So they're rooting for you to succeed!

Want a different approach? The folks in Washington have given you a whole new strategy by passing a shiny new tax law, full of complicated new provisions like the Qualified Business Income rules. If you've never done tax planning before, this is the perfect reason to do it now. And it pre-answers the "why haven't you already done this?" objection because it's the first really major tax change in the last 31 years!

"Mr. Client, you've probably heard that Washington passed a big tax bill last year. There are a lot of goodies in it that you can just sit back and enjoy, like lower tax rates and a bigger Child Tax Credit. But there are a lot of new rules that are going to take some planning to take advantage of, like the new Qualified Business Income rules. So it's time for us to sit down and do a formal tax plan. The cost will be $x,xxx. And I know you don't want to pay that much. But it's tax-deductible, and I'm pretty sure I'll save you at least twice that amount in first year taxes. So, what do you say?"

Now, here's the key. You aren't just going to look at the new tax law rules. You're going to look at everything. It's like when you take your car to the mechanic for a leaking radiator hose. If he lifts the hood and sees a busted alternator cable, do you want him to ignore it because that's not why you brought the car in? Of course, not–you want him to fix that, too. So, you're going to use the new tax law as the rationale for opening the hood . . . but once you get underneath, you're going to fix whatever needs fixing!

Finally, if you're a financial advisor, selling existing clients should be even easier because you don't have to be afraid of making the "old" you look bad. You don't even have to get them to fire their current accountant! The conversation might sound like this:

"Mr. Client, I want to thank you for the chance to handle your insurance/investment/financial business over the past few years. I've enjoyed working with you, and I'm proud of the work that I've done.

Now, I'm not a CPA, and I don't prepare tax returns for my clients. But I've come to realize over time that many of my clients are paying more taxes than they have to. Their accountants do a great job of putting the right numbers in the right boxes on the right forms. But most of them don't have time to sit down with everyone and do any comprehensive planning.

So, I've decided to add comprehensive planning to my service. And I think it's perfect for you. (At this point, you'll go into the "Explain How it Works," "Explain Your Role," and "Pivot to the Disclaimer" steps from the five-part system for opening cases.)

The fee for the service is $x,xxx. And I know you don't want to pay $x,xxx. But it's tax-deductible, of course. And I guarantee you'll save at least twice the fee in the first year alone, or I'll give you a complete refund.

You get the idea. Selling tax-planning services to current clients involves leveraging the trust they already place in you and explaining why your new service is an extension of what they're already engaging you to provide.

Establishing Your Value to Your Clients

"When it comes to finances, remember there are no withholding taxes on the wages of sin."

Mae West

Now let's talk about just how much your tax-planning service is worth. The Tax Master Network® offers members a helpful motto, in genuine Latin, to help them remember. It's lucror vestri dignitas, and it means "charge what you're worth." But how do you know what you're worth so that you can go about charging for it?

For generations, accountants and attorneys have tracked their time and billed their clients accordingly. And that may have been fine – generations ago. (Announcer voice: "it wasn't.") Hourly billing should have died back in the Mad Men era. But accountants as a group are conservative and reluctant to change; they sometimes hold on to tradition too long. And financial advisors, even though their profession generally adapts to change faster than accounting, sometimes have trouble asking for fees outside a conventional AUM or commission environment.

Here's the problem. Hourly billing rewards you for input and effort. But the amount of time you put into a problem, multiplied by a fixed hourly rate, has nothing to do with the value of solving that problem. This is especially true for tax planning. Tax planning isn't about delivering hours. It's about delivering value.

One Tax Master Network® member tells a story about sitting down with a prospect who was about to retire from a major consumer-goods company. During the course of that hour-long conversation, our member identified a strategy that would save the client a million dollars in federal income tax in that single year. Now, tell me how much he should have charged for that hour? $300? $3,000? $30,000?

(We took that exact scenario to a Facebook group for accountants and asked how much they would charge. One CPA, bless her heart, told us she would charge her regular hourly rate and hope for some referrals. If you're a Southerner, you know exactly what "bless her heart" means. There's a reason some people just don't belong in business for themselves.)

That's really the key. If you want to survive where technology threatens your peers and thrive in a competitive market, you've got to give your clients something beyond billable hours, you've got to stop being a white-collar factory worker. You've got to give them something they can't get anywhere else. And if you want to charge more for your service, you've got to be worth more. (This is true whether you want to charge more than your competitors, or more than your old self.)

That all sounds hard. The good news is, tax planning makes it a lot easier. Why? Because it's so much easier to quantify your value than with any other service you offer!

DECODING THE TAX CODE

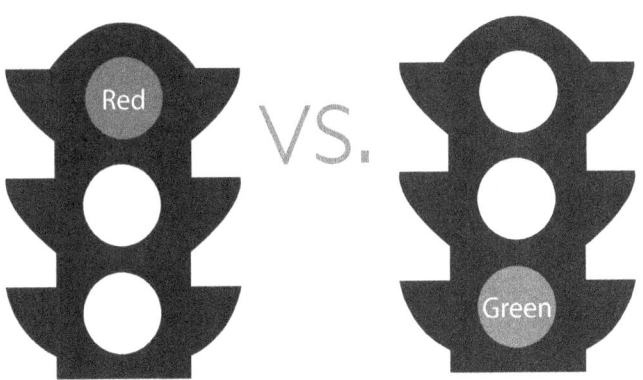

We'll start with another analogy that frames your value in a matter of minutes and immediately sets you apart from the herd. (Have you realized yet how much we love analogies?)

John's Note: Ed and I are analogy machines. Read or listen to anything we write or speak, and you'll find it riddled with anal-

ogies, and we freely take and alter each other's analogies. No real content here, just a fun fact.

You've heard of the Infinite Monkey Theorem, right? Give an infinite number of monkeys an infinite number of typewriters, and sooner or later, one of them will bang out the complete works of William Shakespeare.

Do you know what sort of gibberish they're banging out when they're not banging out Shakespeare? The tax code, of course. There's a reason former President Jimmy Carter once called it "a disgrace to the human race."

So let's help clients make some sense out of the much-maligned code. We're going to position the entire thing–all 2,600+ pages of it–as a series of red lights and green lights. The red lights are where your clients have to stop and pay tax; the green lights are where they don't.

The Tax Code, Decoded

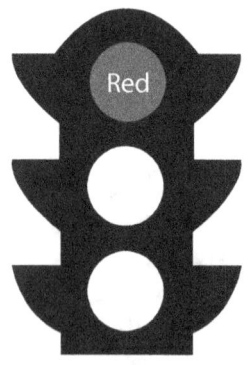

Tax Imposed
(a) **MARRIED INDIVIDUALS FILING JOINT RETURNS AND SURVIVING SPOUSES**
There is hereby imposed on taxable income –
(1) every married individual (as defined in section 7703) who makes a single return jointly with his spouse under section 6013, and
(2) every surviving spouse (as defined in section 2(a)), a tax determination in accordance iwith [the tax table]

Look at the very first page of the Code, Section 1(a): Tax Imposed.

"There is hereby imposed on the taxable income of every married individual (as defined in section 7703) who makes a single return jointly with his spouse under section 6013, and every surviving spouse–as defined in section 2(a)–a tax determined in accordance with [the tax table]."

It's pretty straightforward. Joint filers owe tax, and here's how much. We can call that a red light. Stop and pay tax. Section 1(b), 1(c), and 1(d) go on to lay out the rates for single filers, heads of households, and separate filers, respectively.

Section 1401 imposes the self-employment tax and sets the rate. That's another red light.

Section 1411 imposes the net investment income tax on incomes over $200,000 (single filers) or $250,000 (joint filers). That's another red light.

The Tax Code, Decoded

101: Certain Death Benefits
(a) **PROCEEDS OF LIFE INSURANCE CONTRACTS PAYABLE BY REASON OF DEATH**
(1) GENERAL RULE
Except as otherwise provided in paragraph (2) subsection (d), subsection (f), and subsection (j), gross income does not include amounts received (whether in a single sum or otherwise) under a life insurance contract, if such amounts are paid by reason of the death of the insured.

But the code includes more than just the obvious red lights. There are green lights, too. Take Code Section 101, for example, which says that life insurance death benefits are generally nontaxable. Any time you see the words "gross income does not include, "you're seeing a green light.

And then:

- Code Section 105(b) provides that "gross income does not include" employer-provided health benefits.
- Code Section 162 says "there shall be allowed as a deduction," ordinary and necessary business expenses. When you

see the words "there shall be allowed as a deduction," you're seeing a green light.

- Code Section 170 says "there shall be allowed as a deduction," any charitable contribution (verified under "regulations prescribed by the Secretary.")

- Code Section 179 says that any qualifying business property the taxpayer chooses not to expense "shall be allowed as a deduction."

We could go on for page after page after page. As former Senator Warren Magnuson once said, "the first nine pages of the Internal Revenue Code define income; the remaining 1,100 pages spin the web of exceptions and preferences."

Oh, and just to make things even more fun, don't forget that you can turn right on a red light! What's the tax equivalent? Let's say your client is single, age 40, nets $200,000 from his business and wants to put $30,000 into a Roth IRA. He can't do that, of course. His AGI is well above the limit for contributing (a red light), and even if it's not, contributions are limited to $5,500 per year (another red light). But . . . he can put $30,000 into a SEP and immediately convert that to a Roth. That strategy, also known as a "backdoor Roth" or "Roth SEP," lets your client make a right turn on a red light!

Here's the bottom line: the explanation that sets you apart from anyone else your client has worked with:

"Most accountants, when they look at their clients' taxes, focus on the red lights. And that's important! Blowing through the red lights is how you get in trouble, so they want to keep you out of trouble.

But the tax code actually has more green lights than red lights. And if you just look out for the reds, you miss all those opportunities to save with the green!"

That's why we want to focus on proactive tax planning. Yes, we'll tell clients when they need to stop. But we'll also look for those green lights that most accountants miss—or don't even bother looking for! And we'll let clients know why focusing on the green lights makes us different from our competitors and more valuable than our competitors.

This analogy can even help a financial advisor position himself as more valuable than an accountant! Realistically, the first thing most prospects will ask when you say you do tax planning is, "are you a CPA?" The red light/green light analogy gives you an easy way to say, "No, I'm not, and here's why that's a good thing."

Brand and Positioning

Focusing on the green lights helps solve the biggest problem you face in a crowded marketplace. Prospects don't know how you're different from your competitors, at least not until you educate them. They see you all as a big bushel of apples, and subject you to all sorts of unflattering apples-to-apples comparisons.

If you're a CPA, and your prospect thinks that you, the CPA across the street, the EA around the corner, and the H&R Block office in a crappy strip mall across town all offer the same service, you've got some work to do to set yourself apart. If your prospect thinks that you, the CPA across the street, the EA around the corner, and that H&R Block office (probably wedged between a tattoo parlor and a payday lender) all deliver the same value, you're toast.

Sure, you could try to win those apples-to-apples comparisons. We're faster! We're cheaper! We're open later! But that sets off a race to the bottom where nobody wins. (Somebody's always hungrier or more desperate than you.) And if you're reading this book, it's not because you set out to compete with the H&R Blocks of the world—or the legions of CPAs and EAs competing with H&R Block because they don't know any better.

Here's a better idea. Opt out of those apples-to-apples comparisons entirely. How? Be an orange. Now you don't even have to care what the apples do, or how fast they turn around a return, or how late they're open, or how much they charge.

Client:"My last accountant only charged $600 for my return."

You:"Your last accountant probably did a perfectly good job preparing your return. But that's all they did. I don't just record the history you give me. I help you write it. And the savings I create will more than cover the difference in fees."

There are lots of ways you can become an orange. Most of them involve specializing. You can be a CPA who just happens to work with real estate agents. Or you can be the only CPA in your city who specializes in helping top-performing agents minimize the tax on their commissions. (We know which CPA we'd rather work with.) You can be a financial advisor who has some doctor clients. Or you can be the only advisor in your region who specializes in helping physicians manage their wealth after selling their practice to a larger group or hospital. (Who would you rather work with?)

> *John's Note: One way to become an "orange" is to never bill for hours or forms, but with a monthly membership model. Financial Gravity built a bigger accounting practice, faster than virtually all the accountants reading this book. We did it without the CPA initials, and we did it all with monthly recurring billing. This is outside the scope of the book, but part of the Tax Master Network® business model.*

Your ultimate goal should be to become a category of one. You don't even have any competition. If clients want the particular value you offer, they come to you for it, or they just don't get it at all.

Quantify Your Value

$$\frac{d}{dx}\left[\frac{f(x)}{g(x)}\right] = \frac{g(x)f'(x) - f(x)g'(x)}{g(x)^2}$$

Here's the key to making this all work. You have to quantify your value to your clients, so that you can sit down and explain to them, in cold hard dollars and cents, exactly how much your service is worth.

Conceptually, it's easy. How much money have you saved your client? How much self-employment tax would they have paid as a sole proprietor, versus the FICA they pay as an S corporation? How much can they save investing in a life insurance contract instead of a taxable portfolio? How much can they save by investing in a separate managed account instead of a traditional mutual fund? Add those numbers up and you're done.

The real challenge is to change your mindset to look for those savings, take note of them, do the analysis to quantify them, and record them to communicate to yourself and your clients. It's ok nobody taught this to you in school. You didn't learn it when you interned for a Big Eight firm (if you're old enough) or a Final Four firm (if you're a Millennial).

Make quantifying your value a habit. Create systems to calculate it, record it, and communicate it. We guarantee the effort will pay off in the form of happier clients, more referrals, and an overall better business life.

Communicate Your Value

Once you've quantified your value, the next equally-essential step is to communicate it to your client. Your clients come to you for "the numbers," right? This is true whether it's their business books and records or their investment account statements So how the hell are they going to know what you're worth if you don't tell them? We can promise you no one else will do it!

This is actually really easy for an accountant to do, which makes it a shame that so few of them do it. Just tell them how much your client would have paid before you worked your magic, and how much your smart planning saved them.

Here's a quick example. Let's say your client is a real estate agent netting $100,000 on a Schedule C. You spot an opportunity to use an S corp to cut her employment tax. You settle on a salary of $50,000.

Next year, you'll sit down to prepare her new 1120S and 1040. You'll print out the 1040 and see a bottom line for "total tax."

Want to conjure up a little magic? Make a duplicate copy of her 1040 in your software. Delete the W2 wage and K1 income. Then take both figures and enter them on a Schedule C, and wait for the software to calculate the appropriate self-employment tax on the combined amount. Print out the first two pages of that return, too.

Now, when you sit down with your client, you can show her both returns. The "before" version shows them what they would have paid before your planning. The "after" version shows them their real bill. Simply take the difference, and you'll see exactly how much your planning was worth. (Feel free to adjust that number down by the cost of running payroll and preparing the 1120S.)

This is especially powerful because the client sees both the "before" and "after" numbers on actual tax returns. They don't just hear you report a number and decide to trust you or not. They see both numbers, before and after, in all their black and white glory. It's a powerful and unarguable demonstration of your value.

Presenting the number is a great start. But do you remember in the last chapter, when we told you to confront your client with the cost of the mistakes and missed opportunities that were leading to tax bills they didn't have to pay, and we suggested asking what they would do with that money if they didn't have to waste it on taxes?

The same principle works when you're presenting your value. If you can frame it in emotional terms, you'll earn even more credit. If the client has a daughter in college, saving $25,000 in tax is probably enough to pay a semester of her school. One Tax Master

Network® member tells a story about how his planning saved a client enough to pay for her daughter's wedding. You can be sure that she was a loyal client for life!

YOU ARE THE VALUE

You don't want the client to perceive the value as coming from the plan/solution itself.

You want the client to perceive the value as coming from your delivery of the plan/solution

Finally, remember that in the end, the real value comes from you and not just the planning you do. You don't want the client to perceive the value as coming from the plan itself. You want the client to perceive the value as coming from your delivery of the plan. In the end, the value you deliver through tax planning is a vehicle to make you more valuable and cement your overall relationship with the client. Remember, tax planning can lead to just about any other accounting or financial service you want it to.

Building your **Confidence**

We've mentioned a couple of times that novice tax planners sometimes worry they don't have the technical chops to succeed with their new business. In our experience, nothing builds confidence faster than realizing just how much you're already worth for your clients.

Here's an exercise to get you thinking along those lines. Sit down with a piece of paper or spreadsheet and identify your five most valuable clients. Make a list of every idea you've given them, and how much those ideas have been worth. If the savings repeat, like converting a client from a sole prop to an S corporation, total each year of savings. Now add them all up.

We guarantee you'll be amazed at how much you've already done for your clients without even realizing it. You're already doing this. You just need to start taking credit for it.

Value Pricing for Tax Planning

Ok, we opened this chapter by mocking the dinosaurs who still organize their lives around billable hours and timesheets. Hopefully, you've seen that the time you put into creating a plan, multiplied by some arbitrary fixed hourly rate, bears no relation to the value the client gets out of it. So . . . how the hell do you price a tax planning engagement to reward yourself for the value you create without pushing the client away?

First, consider the fee in the context of the overall client relationship. If you're an accountant and all your revenue comes from traditional fee-for-service billings, an up-front planning fee is probably a pretty important addition to your revenue. But if you're a financial advisor, and the majority of your income derives from commissions or assets under management, an up-front planning fee may be less important than those income streams. In fact, you may even want to waive the fee entirely in order to keep it from standing in the way of those greater amounts. (If you do, you should at least assign a value to the service–say, $3,000–and get credit for waiving it rather than giving away a free service that the client won't value as much simply because there's no price attached.)

Consider establishing tiers of service at different prices for similarly situated clients. For example, you might offer three levels that look like this:

- a "startup" plan for someone looking to structure their retirement portfolio or just launching a new business venture, for $2,000

- an "established business" plan for a mature, profitable business, for $4,000
- a "complex business" plan for someone with multiple businesses or a complicated investment portfolio, for $6,000.

In any case, the fee you charge should be a fraction of the savings you deliver. It's up to you to determine that fraction. But we see Tax Master Network® members routinely charging up to 50% of first-year savings, which works out to 10% over a five-year period.

Here's how financial Gravity structures planning fees:

- We start by using a proprietary spreadsheet to estimate the amount of tax we can save. (This spreadsheet is available to Tax Master Network® members.)
- We divide the savings by two, and round them down to the nearest 1,000.
- We charge the resulting amount, and cap the fee at $10,000. Thus, there are ten possible fees: $1,000, - $10,000.
- At any of those levels, we guarantee the client will save twice their fee in the first year, or we'll revisit the plan to guarantee the client gets the savings we promise.
- If you caught that there are actually 10 possible fees, give yourself a gold star. We have a concession for startups (they can't save money on past mistakes, and we would like to help them avoid them from the start, right!?) We charge $1000 and we don't guarantee a 2X savings.

That structure leaves some money on the table with clients who save far more than $20,000 per year. In fact, our average client saves twelve times their fee in taxes. But that's fine. Our clients are happy, and we benefit from multiple income streams once we implement their plans.

If you're afraid of leaving money on the table, you can always adjust your regular numbers up to reflect extraordinary value. One Tax Master Network® told us he had a client best suited for his top-tier plan, which he usually priced at $7,500. "But then I ran the numbers to see how much I was saving him," he reported, "and I just couldn't do it at $7,500, so I charged him $12,500."

Some members have charged enormous fees in cases where they've delivered enormous value. One member found a group of four partners who brokered a transaction with a $100 million commission. She charged each of those members $50,000 for planning. That may sound like highway robbery. But she saved them over $6 million in taxes. So ask yourself, who got robbed?

It's also worth remembering that there are several stages in the overall process where you can credibly charge separate fees for different kinds of service:

1. You can charge an up-front planning fee for the plan itself–the "prescription." (Doctors charge fees for writing prescriptions they don't fill themselves. Why shouldn't you?)

2. You can charge a one-time implementation fee to implement the strategies you propose. Most plans involve discrete steps like establishing a new business entity, setting up a medical expense reimbursement plan, or hiring and supervising a vendor for a cost-segregation study.

3. Finally, you can charge ongoing fees to keep the balls in the air once you've set them in motion. This might include managing payroll and books for a new S corporation, preparing split-income trust returns for a charitable lead trust, and similar ongoing responsibilities.

The point here is that you don't have to collect all your chips up front. If you get into a plan and discover some sort of enormous opportunity you missed when you priced it, you can usually find some way to make it up on the back end.

John's Note: We can make a pretty good case for capping your fees at the planning stage. If all you're ever going to make on the client who saves $6,000,000 in taxes is your fee, then swing for the fences–charge $50,000, you deserve it! But, if you're going to manage those tax savings ($60k per year in AUM fees) or work on a wealth transfer plan (huge fees and commissions with additional tax savings for the client), you'll find that ongoing relationship to be far more valuable than a mere planning engagement.

Finally, you should be comfortable enough with whatever fee you propose to quote it confidently to your prospect. If you've just eye-balled their return and pulled a number out of your pants, hoping you've figured out the most the traffic will bear, you'll be nervous and uncertain. And it will show. (Prospects can smell fear, you know–it's an evolutionary advantage.) That's where some sort of standardized fee structure saves your bacon.

Practice it in front of a mirror if you have to. Practice it until you can quote it with a straight face. Practice it until your prospect sees you quote it with such confidence that they think everyone invests four-figure and five-figure fees in tax-planning services–so, of course, they should, too.

What if prospects balk? What if they say your fee is too high? Here's an easy response that takes advantage of the fact that you're creating a "category of one" position for yourself:

> Prospect: "Your fee is too high."
> You: "Compared to what?"

Think about this for a minute. If you've priced yourself properly, you're asking your prospect to pay you far less than the tax they'll pay without your planning. That's the only relevant comparison. It doesn't matter how your fees compare to another CPA or financial advisor. How can they, when other CPAs and financial advisors don't even offer the service you're pitching?

In the end, you're not even asking prospects to give up something they aren't already giving up! You're just giving them a choice to pay a smaller amount to you, or a larger amount to the IRS.

John's Note: "You're just giving them a choice to pay a smaller amount to you, or a larger amount to the IRS." I had to repeat it because it's that important. They're paying a multiple of your fee to the IRS. In fact, they really aren't even paying your fee, the IRS is. And when they pay your fee, THAT is even tax deductible! That quote is so important it deserves a box, I cus-tomized it for you. It's like a 'done for your' quote. Memorize it.

"I'm just giving you a choice to pay a smaller amount to me, or a larger amount to the IRS." - You

Tax Strategy Survey

"The hardest thing in the world to understand is the income tax"

- Albert Einstein

This is a book on **selling** tax savings, not creating tax savings. But we know you may not be familiar with the broad range of strategies you can use to make yourself a hero to your clients. So now we'll focus on some specific planning situations where you can show clients how conventional wisdom can actually cost your clients taxes they don't have to pay. These include tax deferral, retirement income planning, insurance products, and mutual funds.

> *John's Note: I'd point out that Ed has several technical guides to creating actual tax savings, including the best-selling book on the new law, that you can find at www.thenewtaxlawbook.com. If you join the Certified Tax Master® program, you'll even have the opportunity to co-brand books on specific strategies including retirement planning, exit strategies, charitable planning, planning for "the 1%," and planning for real estate.*

Before we get started, let's outline some broad tax-planning themes. Earlier, we said the tax code is like a series of red lights and green lights. Those green lights fall into four broad categories: timing, shifting, code, and product. Most accountants are familiar with timing, shifting, and code-based strategies, and less familiar with product-based strategies. Most investment advisors are comfortable with product-based strategies, but less familiar with the first three buckets. (This is what leads to the "hammer-nail problem" we discussed in the first chapter.)

Keys to **Cutting Tax**

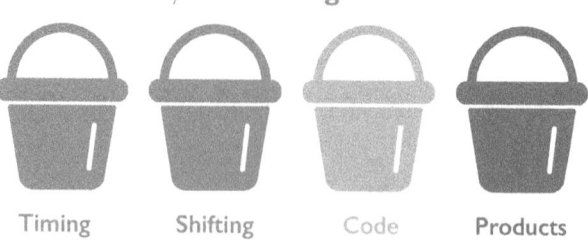

| Timing | Shifting | Code | Products |

- Timing-based strategies generally defer taxes to future dates to take advantage of lower future rates or simply the time value of money. These include most qualified retirement plans and IRAs, installment sales, deferred annuities.
- Shifting-based strategies move taxes from one taxpayer to a lower-bracket taxpayer. These include hiring children to work in a parent's business (subjecting the income to tax at the children's lower rate), using gift-leasebacks to shift income from a business owner to a lower-bracket relative, and using C corporations to shift income away from a client's personal return. (The 2017 tax act, of course, has opened up tremendous new possibilities in that area for more on this www.thenewtax-lawbook.com.)
- Code-based strategies include specific code sections offering specific tax breaks. These include the section 121 exclusion for gains from the sale of a primary residence, the so-called "Augusta Rule" that lets you rent your home to your business for up to 14 days of tax-free income, and charitable remainder trusts for selling appreciated assets without paying tax on those gains.
- Finally, product-based strategies let you take advantage of lower rates or other breaks for specific investment products. These include all sorts of investment vehicles: permanent life insurance, oil & gas interests, swap funds, real estate investment trusts, and more.

It helps to understand which category or categories any particular strategy falls into. Clients also appreciate when you can use this sort of shorthand to explain your recommendations. Also, the Tax Blueprint® sorts each strategy recommendation into these four buckets, which reinforces the four strategies and helps the client better understand specifically how the strategy recommended helps them.

Spotlight on Tax Deferral

Lots of tax planning involves deferring tax on various forms of income. This has become conventional wisdom, especially when it comes to saving for retirement. Stuff as much as you can into a deductible retirement plan, take your guaranteed tax break now, enjoy extra compounding on the money you don't pay in taxes, and pay tax on the withdrawals when you're in a lower tax bracket.

There's just one problem with that conventional wisdom. It isn't always true. And when it's not, it can cost clients big-time. So let's walk through the basic concepts to help clients gauge when best to take advantage of their tax deferral opportunities. When should they take the sure thing now? When are they probably better off waiting?

Tax Deferral: **When Do You Pay**

With any investment, there are three places where you may or may not be subject to tax. You can pay (or not) on the seed when the money goes into the investment. You can pay (or not) on the growth. And finally, you can pay (or not) on the harvest, the distribution of the investment.

The perfect investment would let you deduct your seed, avoid tax on the growth, and avoid tax on the harvest. And it would probably have the word "unicorn" somewhere in the prospectus, because it doesn't exist. Sorry. Or it's illegal, so if this is promised, run! Sorry, again.

The worst investment would impose a tax on your seed, your growth, and your harvest. Fortunately, that doesn't exist either. See, the IRS isn't ALL bad.

As for real-world choices?

- Taxable stocks and stock mutual funds give you no break on the seed (because you buy them with after-tax dollars), tax deferral on the price appreciation and lower preferential rates on qualified corporate dividends, and a slight break on the harvest in the form of preferential capital gain rates on sales.

- Traditional IRAs and qualified plans give you a break on the seed (by letting you deduct your contribution) and avoid tax on the growth, but tax you on the distributions at ordinary income rates. That's two out of three (not bad), but with pretty strict contribution limits, penalties for early withdrawals, and required minimum distributions beginning at age 70½. Also, they subject your capital gains to higher rates on ordinary income. Finally, the tax burden transfers at death to heirs who may have an even higher rate.

- Roth IRAs give you no break on the seed, but avoid tax on the growth and the harvest. There may be slight penalties on withdrawals within the first five account years, but no required minimum distributions.

- Life insurance gets no break on the seed, but avoids tax on the growth and, as long as you maintain the policy in force, the harvest can be tax free. It also passes to heirs tax free. (If you're fortunate to have enough to be subject to estate tax, there are ways to pass this outside the estate as well). There are no statutory contribution limits, no penalty for early withdrawals or required minimum distributions. On the downside, depending on your health, the cost of insurance can be a significant stumbling block.

- Non-qualified deferred annuities get no break on the seed. They defer tax on the growth, but there's no break on the harvest. In fact, unless you annuitize the contract, all your gains are taxed under LIFO rules. And if you're buying equities inside a variable annuity or equity-index annuity, you'll convert those capital gains into ordinary income. (If you've noticed that all the other investments we've discussed offer two breaks, but annuities offer only one, then congratulations on paying attention.) They also do not have a step up in cost basis at death, which you would get if you owned the same money in a mutual fund outside the annuity.

John's Note: This goes back to the problem with advisors selling the "three." Fixed Indexed Annuities and Variable Annuities are VERY popular to sell: they pay well, they have a good story, and they promise "tax savings." But the actual savings are weak, at best. Clients can generally do much better elsewhere.

In the end, many annuity sales fall into the "bait and switch" category. The tax savings are the bait, but the products don't really deliver. I wouldn't recommend buying any annuity with non-qualified money. Some annuities make sense as a bond replacement in a diversified portfolio and in qualified accounts, but the annuities that pay the best to agents are typically the worst for clients. Just a word of warning: you'll undo all the goodwill you get from solid tax planning by selling a good product used incorrectly. You'll do even worse by selling a bad product.

So, which break is most valuable? Well, it depends. Where would your client pay the most tax–the seed, the growth, or the harvest? That's where you should take your break!

Unfortunately, it's not always possible to know where your tax bill will be highest. That's because, while you know how much tax you'll pay today, you can't be sure what you'll pay down the road.

The chart below shows top marginal tax rates since the modern income tax first appeared in 1913. The first year had a top rate of 5% on income over $500,000–about $12.6 million in today's dollars. But rates shot up quickly to pay for World War I and went even higher to pay for World War II. (Fun fact: The Wealth Tax Act of 1935, also called the "Soak the Rich" tax, took an extra 75% of income above $5 million and hit just one taxpayer–Standard Oil heir John D. Rockefeller Jr.)

Top Marginal Tax Rates

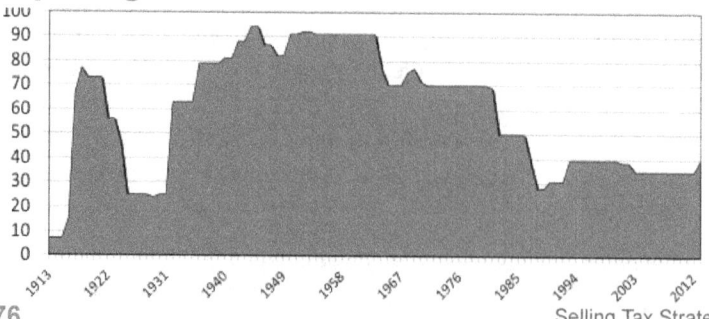

Selling Tax Strategies

The top rate hovered at what today's taxpayers would consider unfathomably high levels until 1981 when the Reagan administration pushed it down to 50%. The Tax Reform Act of 1986 pushed it even lower, and the top federal income tax rate hasn't pushed above 39.6% since then. (Medicare and net investment income taxes mean that some high-income earners may actually pay more.)

More recently, marginal rates have topped out from 35% to 39.6%. That may sound like a big difference for someone wanting to pay less. Who wouldn't think that cutting the top rate from 39.6% in 2017 to 37% in 2018 is a victory? But again, in the broader historical context, we're still on the low end of the scale. Top earners howled when their rate went from 36% to 39.6%. Can you imagine the outcry if they had gone back to 50% like under Reagan? Seventy percent like under Nixon? *Ninety percent* like under Eisenhower? (And those were all *Republican* presidents!)

Now let's add our current fiscal situation to the mix. As we write these words, the federal debt stands at over $20 trillion, and growing by another trillion dollars per year for as long as the eye can see. Which direction are taxes likely to go as a result? Probably up, not down. And we'll probably see new forms of tax, like some sort of carbon tax or value-added tax, to help slow that growth.

As we said earlier, conventional wisdom holds that clients should take their tax deferral while they're in their peak earning years under the assumption that they'll be earning a lower income, thus falling into a lower tax bracket, in retirement. But will that remain true going forward? Maybe . . . but we shouldn't count on it!

This seems a good time to mention that on December 14, 2017, tax professionals didn't know what their clients' tax rates would be just *18 days later* on January 1! If you really think you can know what a client's rate is going to be when they retire in 20 years, might we suggest you get out of whatever business you're in now and start buying lottery tickets?

Clients themselves don't always fit the conventional "lower income in retirement" model. Most clients want to retire with roughly the same spendable income they enjoyed while they were working.

(That's not the same thing as pre-tax income–most retirees can earn less top-line income because they won't have to continue making retirement plan contributions, pay employment tax on their income, or shoulder the costs of commuting, maintaining a professional wardrobe, and kicking in every time a fellow employee gets married or has a baby.)

Many clients even spend more in their first few years of retirement. River cruises down the Rhine are more expensive than commuting, and those grandchildren aren't going to buy cute rompers or start saving for college on their own.

> *John's Note: I've watched and helped many people retire, and I've seen many clients be surprised by the transition. The worst is not recognizing that when you have all that free time from not working, you tend to fill it with stuff that costs money, instead of (when you were working) just going home and crashing on the couch and watching Netflix for $10 a month. It turns out that real traveling is much more expensive than watching the Travel Channel. Who knew?*

In the end, it would be great if we could give you an easy formula to recommend when clients should take their tax savings. It would also be "authorial malpractice," if that really existed. Every case is different. Sometimes you can crunch numbers and point one way or the other. Other times, the best you can do is present the choice to the client and let **them** make the call.

Finally, tax deferral also presents you with two specific ethical dilemmas. First, to what extent can you say that you're **saving** clients tax when you're merely **deferring** them? And second, how can you claim credit for guaranteed savings when you can't specifically quantify them?

Let's say your client hasn't started saving for retirement, and now they're ready to take the plunge. They're making a nice income, in the 24% bracket. You recommend a solo 401(k) with an $18,500 deferral and $15k profit-share contribution for a $33,500 total deduction.

Assuming all $33,500 would have been taxed at 24%, you've just "saved" your client $8,040–plus potential state and local tax as well. That sounds like a home run, right?

Here's the problem. You haven't really *saved* the client that $8,040 at all. You've *deferred* the tax on $33,500. And you've given the client a chance to earn additional income on the $8,040 that would have been paid in taxes.

Someday, that client (or his heirs) is going to wind up paying the tax on that $33,500. And if that "someday" is more than a few years down the road, we have no idea what that tax will be? Will rates be lower? Maybe–after all, that's the conventional wisdom. If our current rate structure stands (which we all know is a pretty big "if"), and the client drops down to the 22% bracket, the ultimate savings on the $33,500 deferral will be just $670. And even then, the time value of money suggests that $670 might not buy much.

Of course, the move creates extra wealth by letting the client invest the money that would have gone to taxes had they been paid up front. But how do you quantify that value without getting into quantum mechanics or multi-variable calculus–especially if the client is a technical/engineering type who really wants you to show your work!?!

At the same time, deferring the savings until tomorrow makes it hard for you to quantify the value of your recommendation when you simply can't know how much tax your client will ultimately avoid–even though you know it will be enormous!

Let's say your client is 50 years old with $200,000 in a traditional IRA. She leaves a $200,000/year job to start a new business and makes nothing her first year of self-employment. You spot the opportunity to use that year of artificially low income to convert the traditional IRA into a Roth.

Assuming she files singly and takes the standard deduction, that move will cost her about $42,000. Regardless of her specific circumstances, today's tax bill is easy enough to calculate.

We also know that converting her IRA to a Roth will completely eliminate any future tax on that account. But how can we know how much that's worth? Well, we can't. How fast will the account grow? How long will she wait to start taking withdrawals? What would the future tax rates be on those withdrawals? What effect would those taxable withdrawals have on the rest of her taxable income? (Remember, her future required minimum withdrawals could subject her Social Security benefits to tax, phase out her medical expense deductions, and boost her Medicare Part B premiums, among other effects.)

Twenty-five years of growth at 10% turns that $200,000 into more than $2 million. It's easy to project the eventual tax burden on that lump sum at a million dollars or more. How does an ethical advisor, who also wants credit for being a hero, quantify credit for that planning victory?

Spotlight on Retirement Income

Once a client hits retirement age, there are two special tax threats to manage. The first, which kicks in when they start collecting Social Security, is avoiding tax on those benefits. The second, which kicks in when they reach age 70½, is managing required minimum distributions, or RMDs.

Tax on Social Security: **Provisional Income**

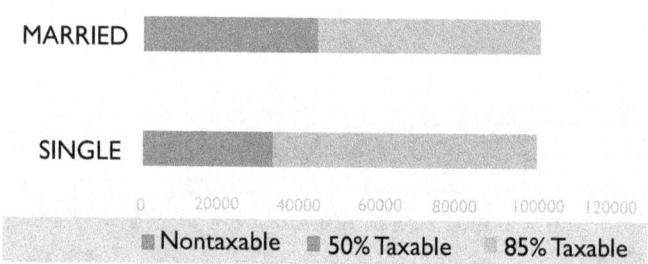

Social Security benefits are nontaxable for about 2/3 of retirees. However, beneficiaries under their full retirement age with earned income face a special penalty tax on their benefits. And beneficiaries of any age face tax on their benefits once their "modified adjusted gross income" (MAGI) reaches certain levels. (MAGI generally equals regular AGI plus otherwise-nontaxable municipal bond interest income plus 50% of Social Security benefits.)

- Clients who file singly with MAGIs over $25,000 owe tax on 50% of their benefit. Once MAGI tops $34,000, they'll owe tax on 85% of their benefit. If their regular AGI is over $85,000, their Medicare Part B and Part D premiums will go up. (The premium increase isn't huge–for 2018, it ranges from $53.50 for participants with AGIs over $85,000 to $294.60 for participants with AGIs over $160,000 for Part B. Still, why pay extra if you don't have to?)

- Clients who file jointly with MAGIs over $32,000 owe tax on 50% of their Social Security. Once MAGI tops $44,000, they owe tax on 85% of their benefit. And if their regular AGI is over $170,000, their Medicare Part B and Part D premiums go up.

Some clients simply make too much money to have any choice in the matter. But other clients whose incomes are closer to those thresholds can benefit from careful planning to avoid that extra tax hit.

Uniform Lifetime Table

For use by:
- Unmarried owners
- Married owner whose spouse is not more than 10 years younger
- Married owner whose spouse is in not the sole beneficiary

Age	Distribution Period	Age	Distribution Period	Age	Distribution Period
70	27.4	85	14.8	100	6.3
71	26.5	86	14.1	101	5.9
72	25.6	87	13.4	102	5.5
73	24.7	88	12.7	103	5.2
74	23.8	89	12.0	104	4.9
75	22.9	90	11.4	105	4.5
76	22.0	91	10.8	106	4.2
77	21.2	92	10.2	107	3.9
78	20.3	93	9.6	108	3.7
79	19.5	94	9.1	109	3.4
80	18.7	95	8.6	110	3.1
81	17.9	96	8.1	111	2.9
82	17.1	97	7.6	112	2.6
83	16.3	98	7.1	113	2.4
84	15.5	99	6.7	114	2.1
				115+	1.9

The next challenge involves managing RMDs from traditional IRA and qualified plan accounts. Those RMDs, force clients to recognize income whether they need it or not. They can wreak havoc on a careful plan to avoid tax on Social Security benefits. In this case, it's unfortunate that the rules are so simple, because that means there's not a lot of wiggle room:

1. The first distribution is due by April 1 of the year after the year in which the client reaches age 70½. The amount is based on the previous year-end account balance, as reported on Form 5498. That distribution counts for the year the client reaches that age. The next distribution is due by December 31 of that same year-end balance, minus the first year's distribution.

2. To calculate distributions going forward, simply divide the previous year's December 31 account balance by the distribution period for your age. If you have more than one account, calculate distributions separately for each account. However, you can take the required total from a single account.

3. If the client's beneficiary is their spouse, and is more than 10 years younger than the client, they can withdraw funds over their true life expectancy as found in IRS Life Expectancy Table II.

You might think it always makes sense to wait as long as possible for taking that first RMD. But waiting until the last minute to do so, and then taking your second required distribution in the same calendar year, means doubling the impact of the RMD, raises the client's AGI for figuring deductions and credits, and may push them into a higher tax bracket. If this is the case, consider taking that required minimum distribution in the year in which the client reaches age 70½ rather than waiting until next April's required beginning date.

And what happens if a client misses an RMD? In that case, they'll owe a special tax equal to 50% of the amount they should have taken. The IRS may waive this tax only if the client shows the shortfall was due to reasonable error and they've taken reasonable steps to remedy the shortfall.

These rules for taxing Social Security benefits and forcing RMDs suggest that paying close attention to managing how retired clients manage their income can pay extra dividends in the form of lower taxes. Here's a framework for understanding and working through that challenge.

"Three Bucket" **Framework**

Taxable Assets	Tax-Deferred Assets	Tax-Free Assets
Stocks, Taxable Bonds, Taxable Funds, etc	Traditional IRAs Qualified Plans Annuities	Roth Accounts Insurance

Clients generally have three ways they can hold assets:

- **Taxable Assets.** They can hold fully taxable assets in their own name (or perhaps a revocable living trust they establish to avoid probate at death). These assets will be taxed under the regular rules for whatever class they fall into. Taxable cash and cash equivalents will be taxable immediately at ordinary income rates; bond interest will be taxed immediately at ordinary income rates, most stock dividends will be taxed at "qualified dividend" rates, long-term capital gains will be taxed at preferential lower rates, etc. These rules will hold true whether the client takes the income for day-to-day spending or reinvests it into their portfolio.

- **Tax-Deferred Assets.** Tax-*deferred* assets include traditional IRAs, qualified plans, and annuities. As we already know, there are no taxes on the growth in these accounts like there can be with fully taxable cash, bonds, and equities. But tax-deferred assets can become ticking tax bombs. At some point, clients or their heirs must start withdrawing assets and paying tax on those distributions, whether they need the cash or not.

- **Tax-Free Assets.** Finally, tax-*free* assets include Roth IRA and qualified plan account balances and permanent life insurance. These don't offer clients any tax deduction going in–but when retirement rolls around, clients love the freedom and flexibility of not having to pay tax on the income they draw!

So, how should your clients hold their assets to avoid pushing their income to levels where their Social Security becomes taxable. How can they minimize or eliminate punitive required minimum distributions? Once they're retired, common sense suggests that tax-free assets are the winner. Helping clients with taxable and tax-deferred assets shift them into tax-free assets becomes a terrific planning opportunity!

There's no single "right" way for clients to allocate their retirement savings; there are simply too many individual considerations to make that possible. Consider these general rules as you work to create your plans:

1. Standard or itemized deductions let clients earn a fair amount of otherwise taxable income from either of the first two buckets before owing any actual tax. (For 2018, this is a minimum of $24,000 for a married couple.) Consider leaving enough in taxable or tax-deferred accounts to maximize this "free allowance."

2. Be sure that clients contribute enough to employer-sponsored plans to qualify for as many matching dollars as possible. This is "free money" they shouldn't pass up, even if it creates future tax challenges down the road.

3. Once they've made the most efficient use of those first two buckets, consider allocating more of their assets to the final tax-free bucket.

4. Take a careful look at any and all opportunities to convert traditional IRA and qualified plan accounts to Roths.

Spotlight on Insurance Products

Life insurance policies that include a cash value offer several significant tax planning opportunities for supplemental or even primary retirement savings. If clients have maxed out available retirement plan contributions, deductible retirement accounts or plans aren't appropriate for their circumstances, or they simply want to invest their savings in a tax-free environment, life insurance may offer a solution. Here are the basic rules:

- Policy cash values grow tax-deferred. Gains aren't taxed unless clients let the policy lapse and cash out for more than they paid in. In that case, their taxable gain equals the cash value withdrawn minus premiums paid.

- Policyholders can take cash from their policy, tax free, by withdrawing their original premiums and borrowing against remaining cash values. They'll pay (nondeductible) interest on the loan but earn it back on the cash value. Many insurers offer "wash loan" provisions with little or no out-of-pocket costs.

Pay close attention to that last point. Your client can buy a life insurance policy, say, at age 40. Stuff $20,000 per year into it for 25 years, for a total of $500,000 in premium. Watch that policy grow to $1 million or more. And take it all tax free, in the form of withdrawals (up to your original $500,000 in premium) then loans. And, so long as they maintain the policy in force, they'll never pay a dime in tax on their "income."

What's more, life insurance loans and withdrawals don't increase "modified adjusted gross income" for purposes of taxing your Social Security benefits. They don't increase AGI, which can phase out deductions for medical expenses or casualty/theft losses. And they aren't subject to the 3.8% "unearned income Medicare contribution" for those earning over $200,000 ($250,000 for joint filers). Not bad!

Unfortunately, these advantages aren't unlimited. Stuff too much cash into the policy in the first seven years and it's considered a "modified endowment contract." Withdrawals will be taxed as ordinary income until the "inside buildup" (the gain above and beyond your original premiums) is gone. (This is sometimes called the "seven-pay" limit because it's pegged at the amount it would take to pay for the policy in full in just seven years.)

Insurance companies offer four main types of cash-value policies for different investors. The key is finding a policy that matches the client's investment temperament:

- "Whole life" resembles a bank CD in a tax-advantaged wrapper, with required annual premiums and strong guarantees.

- "Universal life" resembles a bond fund in a tax-advantaged wrapper, with flexible premiums but less strong guarantees.

- "Variable life" lets policyholders invest cash values in a series of "sub accounts" resembling mutual funds. They can choose "variable whole life" with required premiums and stronger guarantees, or "variable universal life" contracts with flexible premiums and less strong guarantees. "Private placement" contracts for cash values of $500,000 or more can even let clients choose their own managers, rather than settle for an insurance company's lineup of "retail" sub accounts.

- Finally, "equity-index" policies guarantee a minimum fixed return with an option to profit from growth tied to a stock market index. This is a popular alternative to universal life because it gives clients a guaranteed floor and protection against market downturns, plus the chance to profit from equity market gains.

John's Note: I'd add there are hybrids of all the above and insurance companies mix and match these and rename and re-brand them. For example, an "Equity-Index" and a "Fixed-Index" annuity or life policy are the same thing. But, no matter what the name, they fall within the standard four above.

If you decide you want a different type of policy or even just a different insurance company, you can exchange your money from one policy to another, tax free. This is called a "1035 exchange."

"Participating" life insurance policies pay "dividends" out of the company's surplus earnings for the year. Policyholders can take them in cash, leave them with the insurer to earn interest, or use them to buy additional insurance. Regardless of which option they choose, dividends are considered a nontaxable return of their own premiums until the total amount of dividends paid out exceeds their "basis" in the contract (the total amount of premiums paid in). At that point, they're taxable as ordinary income. There's no 20% rate cap as there is on "qualified corporate dividends."

In the end, a life insurance contract is a like a "private Roth IRA," but with no contribution limits, income phaseouts, or penalties on withdrawals within the first five account years.

With all those advantages, you'd think everyone wants life insurance. Well, not quite:

- If you can't benefit from owning the actual death benefit, the cost of paying for the death benefit may outweigh the tax benefits.

- If your health is poor, the cost of insurance may make investing in life insurance unaffordably high.

- High first-year commissions mean it may take some time for significant cash values to accumulate.

Life insurance critics also point to the high commissions as a reason not to buy. It's true that commissions typically run 80-100% of the first year's premium. That sounds like a lot, especially if you compare it to investing with a typical financial advisor charging just 1% of assets under management. But what insurance critics miss is that commission is based on the first-year premium and paid just once–while the advisor collects that 1% on the entire account balance–including contributions and growth–and collects it year after year after year.

Year	Y-E Account Value	1% Fee	Year	Y-E Account Value	1% Fee
1	10,600.00	106.00	16	27,128.80	2,721.29
2	21,836.00	218.36	17	299,056.53	2,990.57
3	33,746.16	337.46	18	327,599.92	3,276.00
4	46,370.93	463.71	19	357,855.91	3.578.56
5	59,753.19	597.53	20	389,927.27	3,899.27
6	73,938.38	739.38	21	423,922.90	4,239.23
7	88,974.68	889.75	22	459,958.28	4,599.58
8	104,913.16	1,049.13	23	489,155.77	4,981.56
9	121,807.95	1,218.08	24	538,645.12	5,386.45
10	139,716.43	1,397.16	25	581,563.83	5,815.64
11	158,699.41	1,586.99	26	627,057.66	6,270.58
12	178,821.38	1,788.21	27	675,281.12	6,752.81
13	200,150.66	2,001.51	28	726,397.98	7,263.98
14	222,759.70	2,227.60	29	780,581.86	7,805.82
15	246,725.28	2,467.25	30	838,016.77	8,380.17

Figures assume $10,000 annual contribution plus 6% net growth

Take a look at the chart above and see how much more a client pays over time under a 1%-of-assets model than with a one-time commission. The chart assumes a conservative 6% annual growth. If the account grows faster, at some point a client will be paying their advisor more every year than they do with that "outrageous" insurance commission. (This may be old news to insurance professionals, but we bet it's eye-opening to the accountants reading this!)

*John's Note: Back to picking on the advisor again. Since they sell only three things, the one who sells an equity-indexed annuity will make the case that the mutual fund salesperson is bad because they're subjecting you to market risk when the annuity gets the "upside of the market without the downside." The mutual fund seller will counter that the huge annuity commission is the only motivating factor. In the end, they're both right and wrong. Therefore, leading with tax planning is more honest. I joke that I use a super-secret tool that accountants and financial advisors both ignore when giving advice. It's called . . . wait for it . . . math! Follow the math of the tax plan! Some of it will lead to insurance; some of it will lead to retirement plans, some of it leads to neither. But it always leads to a better outcome for the client–which, in turn, leads to a better outcome for **you.***

Deferred **Annuity**

- Fixed annuity
- Equity-index annuity
- Varible annuity

Now let's talk about deferred annuities. The concept is pretty simple. Make contributions to the account, and watch them grow tax-deferred. At some point down the road, the insurance company can convert that lump-sum balance into a guaranteed income the annuitant or annuitants cannot outlive. If life insurance is protection against dying too soon (which, of course, it is), an annuity is protection against living too long.

There are three main flavors of annuity. Fixed annuities pay a fixed rate declared by the insurance company that issues the contract. It's sort of like a bank CD in an insurance wrapper. Equity-index (aka fixed index) annuities pay a minimum guaranteed rate, but also give you the chance to profit from gains in a specified equity index. And variable annuities are like a mutual fund family inside an insurance wrapper. (The "insurance" guarantees a minimum benefit when you annuitize the contract.)

The tax treatment is similar to a traditional IRA. Income you earn inside an annuity grows tax-deferred until you take it out. If you're in a variable annuity, transfers between subaccounts are tax free. Like with IRAs and qualified plans, there are penalties for early withdrawals before age 59½, although there are no minimum required distributions. Income withdrawals are taxed as ordinary income and subject to the 3.8% net investment income tax.

Having said all that, annuities offer more flexibility than traditional retirement accounts, at least for money going in. There are no contribution limits as there are with qualified plans and no income phaseouts as there are with traditional or Roth IRAs. In fact, you don't need "earned income" to contribute at all like you do with IRAs or qualified plans.

That sounds pretty appealing at first. But there are two big "buts" that make most annuities a ticking tax time bomb.

First, no matter which flavor of annuity you buy, if you don't annuitize the contract, all withdrawals are taxed as income until you've exhausted your gains and start taking out your principal. This "last-in, first-out" treatment can actually increase tax bills after the deferral period.

Second, all income is taxed at ordinary rates. This makes little difference for investors using a fixed annuity in lieu of a bank CD or bond alternative. But it makes a big difference for investors using equity-index or variable annuities to invest in equity markets. There's no chance to profit from lower capital gains rates or lower qualified dividend rates. And there's no chance to profit from stepped-up basis at death. Putting money into an equity-index annuity or variable annuity equity subaccount essentially means taking long-term capital growth–which is already tax-advantaged–and converting it into ordinary income.

Now, there may be perfectly valid reasons for making this choice. The equity-index contract gives clients stronger growth guarantees, along with protection from losses in market downturns. They may very well decide that those advantages are worth the trade off of higher taxes on equity gains. But clients should at least be aware of the tradeoff!

John's Note: I'm going to go out on a limb here and say that the variable annuity is the worst financial product on the market--and I can make that case with math. There's nothing the variable annuity does that can't be done somewhere else better and cheaper. But, it pays an upfront commission and a trail for the assets under management. It's very hard for advisors not to sell them because nothing competes with it for compensation–it simply pays the best. But if people truly understood these products, no one would carry them or buy them.

An equity-indexed annuity has all the "features" I'm told are so great in the VA, but with none of the massive costs. Variable annuities can cost clients 5% or more all in, per year. I can prove this with a call to the insurance company or with the brochure and prospectus we all ignore.

My stance has led to many arguments with well-intentioned CPAs and financial advisors. But I can't emphasize enough, these products aren't good for clients. They're good for the advisors and the companies that sell them.

This will cost me lots of speaking opportunities, but I don't care. These products suck, you should stop selling them now.

*There are too many things that make plenty of money that will
serve your clients much better.*

I'll climb down off my soapbox now . . . .

Spotlight on Mutual Funds

Many investors do their investing through mutual funds. The Investment Company Institute reports that U.S.-based funds managed $19.2 trillion in assets at year-end 2016, up $1 trillion from
the year before. Why so popular? It's mainly because funds help
investors diversify their investment in cases where they can't afford
a portfolio of properly-diversified individual securities. However,
their structure creates several tax inefficiencies that can weigh
down performance in taxable accounts, especially as they com-
pound over time. We call those inefficiencies Tax Friction:

1. Income dividends consist of income earned by the fund's
   portfolio—bond interest, stock dividends, etc. These are taxable
   immediately, even when investors choose to reinvest them
   back into the fund.

2. Capital gains dividends are profits from sale of fund assets.
   These are generally taxed as long-term capital gains, regardless of how long investors owned their shares. Like income
   dividends, they're also taxable immediately, even when rein-
   vested.

3. Capital gains dividends can force investors to pay tax on gains
   that accumulate before they even buy into the fund.

4. Let's say that on January 1, the XYZ Growth Fund buys Microsplat at $40 per share. On July 1, your client invests in the
   fund when Microsplat trades at $60 per share. On December
   1, the fund sells Microsplat at $80. Your client will get a capital
   gains distribution and owe tax on his or her share of the full
   Microsplat gain, even though the client personally reaps the
   benefit from just half of it.

Capital gains dividends can even force investors to pay tax on
losing positions.

Again, let's say that on January 1, the XYZ Growth Fund

buys Microsplat at $40 per share. On July 1, your client invests in the fund when Microsplat trades at $80 per share. On December 1, the fund sells Microsplat at $60. Your client will get a capital gains distribution and owe tax on his or her share of the fund's $20 gain even though the client's piece of the fund actually lost that much.

So, while funds offer the chance to diversify investments with other shareholders, they can force investors to pay tax based on other shareholders' decisions. That makes it important to look at some specific strategies for minimizing taxes on funds held in taxable accounts, like brokerage accounts and trusts.

- Consider index funds, which aim to passively track indexes such as the S&P 500 or Russell 2000. These funds avoid the frequent buying and selling that rack up taxes with actively managed funds. That's because managers sell only when the fund needs to redeem shares or the underlying index itself changes.

- Consider exchange-traded funds ("ETFs"), closed-end index funds that trade on an established exchange. They offer similar advantages as open-ended index funds. And they trade just like stocks, which lets clients buy and sell throughout the day, use stop orders and limit orders, and short sales. (They'll pay commissions to trade ETFs, and can't automatically reinvest shares like with open-end funds.)

- Consider tax-managed funds, which focus on after-tax returns by avoiding turnover, harvesting tax losses, and selling specific shares to minimize taxable gains. Some also impose early-redemption fees to discourage withdrawals that might force managers to sell shares and realize gains.

Once you've decided what funds you want to buy, make sure to buy and sell them efficiently. Here are six strategies for buying and selling funds in taxable accounts. Several are the same as for individually traded stocks. Others take advantage of the funds' particular operating structure:

1. **Limit turnover.** Frequent turnover whacks profits with each sale. And frequent trading subjects more gains to high ordinary

income rates, rather than favorable long-term gain rates. But that doesn't mean investors should be afraid to walk away from a loser. And they should also consider using tax swaps to convert paper losses into tax savings.

2. **Avoid "buying the dividend."** Funds accumulate capital gains throughout the year, then pay them out on a designated date near the end of the year. Investors who buy shares just before that date owe tax on those gains whether they actually profit from them or not.

3. **Convert dividend income into capital gains.** This is the reverse of avoiding purchases near year-end. When a fund distributes a dividend, the price of each share falls by the dividend distribution. That dividend is taxed as ordinary income, "qualified corporate dividend," or capital gain. If investors want to sell shares that generate interest income that they've held for more than a year, consider doing so when the shares are "fat" before that dividend is paid out. This effectively converts that income, otherwise taxed at ordinary rates, into capital gains, taxed at preferential rates.

4. **Beware check-writing with short-term bond funds.** Many funds let investors redeem shares by simply writing a check. The fund then covers the check directly. Sure, it's convenient. But each time an investor writes a check, they sell shares with different holding periods and cost bases. And investors can't specify which shares to sell. (The fund prospectus tells which shares will be liquidated.) This doesn't necessarily mean throwing away the checkbook–just understand the recordkeeping hassles it creates.

5. **Beware systematic withdrawals.** These plans pay specific dollar amounts monthly or quarterly. Fund managers will finance those payments with accumulated income first, then liquidates shares if that accumulated income isn't enough to pay the entire distribution. Like check-writing, this forces investors to sell shares at different times and different prices. Confining systematic withdrawals to tax-deferred accounts avoids a lot of paperwork.

6. **Be careful with portfolio rebalancing.** Most investors start with an overall asset allocation of stocks, bonds, and cash,

before drilling down to pick individual funds. Portfolio rebalancing plans periodically buy and sell those funds to maintain that original target asset allocation. The problem here is that rebalancing forces investors to sell winners (thus recognizing gains), to generate cash to replenish laggards. Investors should consider replenishing the lagging funds with new money, rather than from selling their winners. They also should consider confining their "rebalancing" transactions within your tax-deferred accounts.

The mutual fund model even forces non-tax costs on investors. Funds have to be ready to cash out investors at any moment. This means they have to keep a portion of their assets in low-yield cash or cash equivalents. This "cash drag" can significantly reduce your return over time.

John's Note: This means an S&P 500 fund is NEVER fully invested in the S&P 500. It may only be 90% invested in the 500 stocks. So the low cost is not as low as you thought. (In fact, it's worse, but that's a topic for another book.) We do help our accountants and advisors highlight these inefficiencies by teaching Factor-Based Investing® and by outlining the many inefficiencies in portfolios with the Wealth Blueprint.

The best strategy for taxable clients may be to avoid funds entirely and use separately managed accounts, or "SMAs." These accounts are mutual fund alternatives that give clients the tax advantages of holding individual securities rather than a piece of a fund. One study pegs the cost of tax friction at 1.4% per year, a cost eliminated in an SMA.

Remember, with ordinary mutual funds, investors choose a manager then pay cash for a piece of the fund itself. A hired manager directs the fund, which owns the underlying investments. With SMAs, in contrast, investors choose a manager then give them cash or securities to open a separate account of their own. The manager directs the portfolio, and the investor owns the actual securities individually. Here are the benefits:

- Most importantly, you're "out of the pool." It simply doesn't matter what other investors do with their investments. They don't have to worry, for example, if the market drops and fellow shareholders want to cut and run, which would force the manager to sell underlying shares and possibly realize capital gains to distribute to investors who choose to stay through the correction or even buy on the dip.

- Investors have flexibility to limit turnover, match gains and losses, and even take advantage of tax swaps.

- Investors can use an SMA as a "completion fund" to complement a significant position in a single stock. An investor who retires from Proctor & Gamble, for example, may have millions of dollars in that stock. The last thing they need is a mutual fund that buys them more. They may even want to avoid the entire consumer goods sector. SMAs let investors direct their manager to avoid duplicating those sorts of undiversified positions.

- Investors looking to make charitable gifts can direct their manager to make gifts of specific securities for even more flexibility.

Where to Go from Here

"The income tax has created more criminals than any other single act of government."

Barry Goldwater

So . . . what do you think?

Do you like what you've just read? Does it resonate with you?

Do you agree that the traditional accounting industry fails to serve clients who want more than just recording history and tax returns? Do you see how advancing technology threatens those businesses?

Do you see how proactive tax planning can open doors to business for accountants, tax professionals, and financial advisors alike?

Do you see how easy it can be to attract prospects, open cases, and close sales?

Do you see the impact this can have on the lives of your clients and on your business?

Dip Your Toe into the Water

If you're impressed enough with what you've read to do something about it, your first step should be to check out the Tax Master Network®.

The Tax Master Network® offers a diverse community of progressive tax and finance professionals, looking to harness the power of proactive tax planning to build their business. You'll find software to prepare plans, marketing tools, and templates to attract prospects, sales strategies to turn them into clients, and implementation guides and tools to manage the ongoing business.

You'll also find weekly and monthly group master-minding webinars and regional and national meetings where you can network with fellow planners. Our weekly email is free. Memberships start as low as $49 per month. Our top-level program even includes recruiting and managing a local salesperson to generate clients on your behalf!

Visit www.TaxMasterNetwork.com for all of these benefits and more!

The Fractional Family Office®

The Declaration of Independence famously states that "all men are created equal." But that's not the case when it comes to financial services. Clients at different levels in the financial food chain don't all have access to the same levels of tax and financial planning services. There's nothing wrong with that, of course. Most middle-income clients with jobs and 401(k)s don't need the sort of sophisticated planning and services that high-net-worth clients with multiple business interests and complex investment portfolios do. But if you're looking to build a practice in those fields, it makes sense to understand the competitive landscape and make a conscious decision where you want to position yourself. Here at Financial Gravity, we've created a concept we call the Fractional Family Office® that may intrigue you.

Joe Sixpack manages an assembly line down at the local plant. His wife, Jane, is a school nurse. The family has joint checking and savings accounts and a mortgage at the local bank. Joe invests his retirement savings in mutual funds through his 401(k), and his wife invests in a different set of funds through her 403(b). They bought term life insurance from an online agent after listening to a radio commercial featuring a washed-up 70s actor. They take their taxes to H&R Block. And they went online to LegalZoom.com for wills.

There's nothing wrong with any of those providers or services. Plenty of firms have made money serving Middle America's financial needs. You can become one of them, too, if you're willing to focus on volume rather than value. (But go back and re-read the first chapter to learn why you shouldn't.)

Moving up the financial ladder, Jane Beeper is a successful physician in private practice. She deals with the same bank as the Sixpacks, but she uses their private banking service, which offered her a jumbo loan on her new house. She sponsors a SIMPLE IRA at work and invests her taxable money in separate managed accounts. She bought an equity-index life policy from an agent she met at her country club. She does her accounting and tax work with a partner at a local firm. And the attorney who drafted her trust and will is a partner at a downtown white-shoe firm.

This is probably where you want to be. The problem is, so do most of your competitors! How can you stand apart from the crowd to win Dr. Beeper's business?

At the top of the financial food chain, Thurston Howell III is a day-drinking third-generation heir of a Gilded Age potash mining fortune. Thurston couldn't tell you where he banks, or does his investing, or who does his taxes, if his life depended on it. Instead, he and his equally dissolute siblings have a family office that manages all those pesky "details" for them. The office and staff manage the heirs' rapidly-dwindling portfolios, along with the tax, accounting, and legal work necessary to keep them afloat. They also hire and fire the household help. If Howell's 17-year-old granddaughter crashes her Porsche, someone from the office runs down to the dealer to pick up a new one, in the same color (because god forbid Princess doesn't have her Porsche). And if Princess gets into any serious trouble, well, someone else at the family office "knows a guy."

Few of us would want to get caught up with Thurston Howell and his dysfunctional clan. But many of us would love to offer that level of service to our clients. The problem, of course, is that establishing and maintaining a family office is prohibitively expensive. It's generally reserved for those with $30-50 million or more to invest.

But what if there were a way that you could offer that sort of service to your clients, without the eight-figure price tag? That's where the Fractional Family Office® comes in.

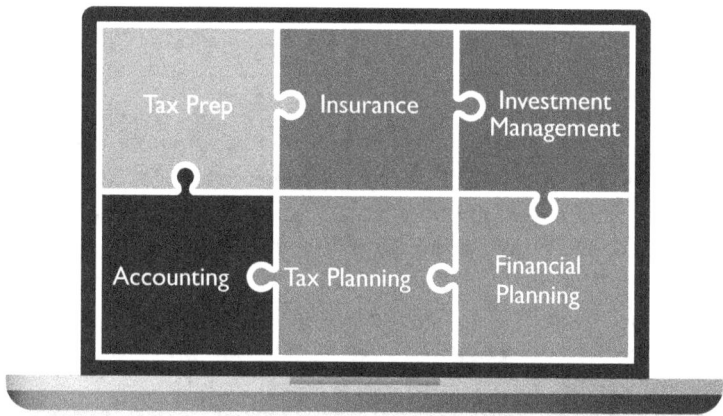

Affluent business owners generally benefit from six major services. They typically get those services from providers in two broad areas:

- Typically, CPAs provide accounting and tax prep. (We know that clients also want tax planning, and aren't getting it. That's why tax planning is such an effective door opener to the rest of these services.) Many CPAs are now also moving into insurance, investing, and financial planning.

- Insurance agents offer insurance, financial planners offer planning advice, and investment managers run the money.

These days, many if not most financial advisors look to provide all three of those services. Some of them are now dipping their toes into the tax waters.

Family offices give ultra-high-net-worth clients all of these services under one umbrella. (They may outsource specific functions, like tax planning or tax prep, but they serve as a single point of contact and hub for all of the services.) Family offices also focus special attention on building their clients' legacies, through educating the family children and grandchildren about the responsibilities of wealth and even stepping in to help elevate them from "donors" to true "philanthropists."

Financial Gravity currently provides all six of those services to business owners and individual investors across the country from our headquarters in suburban Dallas. If you offer one or more yourself–and you'd like to offer the rest–you can "plug in" Financial Gravity as your outsourced provider for any of the others you're not currently offering yourself. This lets you become the "hub" or "quarterback," just like the family office.

Many of you are familiar with "outsourced CFO" services. The Fractional Family Office® harnesses the same principle, just for a different type of service.

Or . . . if you must . . . you can think of the Fractional Family Office® as "Uber for family offices." There. We said it.

If you'd like more information about working with Financial Gravity and putting the Fractional Family Office® to work, visit us at www.financialgravity.com

Questions and Notes